Voter Suppression
in U.S. Elections

HISTORY
IN THE HEADLINES

Voter Suppression
in U.S. Elections

EDITED BY Jim Downs

The University of Georgia Press   *Athens*

© 2020 by the University of Georgia Press
Athens, Georgia 30602
www.ugapress.org
All rights reserved
Designed by Erin Kirk
Set in Garamond Premier Pro and ITC Franklin Gothic
Printed and bound by Sheridan Books
The paper in this book meets the guidelines for
permanence and durability of the Committee on
Production Guidelines for Book Longevity of the
Council on Library Resources.

Most University of Georgia Press titles are
available from popular e-book vendors.

Printed in the United States of America
24   23   22   21   20   P   5   4   3   2   1

Library of Congress Cataloging-in-Publication Data

Names: Downs, Jim, 1973– editor. | University of Georgia. Press
Title: Voter suppression in U.S. elections / edited by Jim Downs.
Other titles: Voter suppression in United States elections | History in
   the headlines (Athens, Ga.)
Description: Athens : The University of Georgia Press, 2020. | Series:
   History in the headlines | Includes bibliographical references.
Identifiers: LCCN 2020006563 | ISBN 9780820357737 (Hardback) |
   ISBN 9780820357744 (Paperback) | ISBN 9780820357751 (eBook)
Subjects: LCSH: Suffrage—United States—History. | Voting—
   United States—History. | Voter registration—Corrupt
   practices—United States—History. | Elections—Corrupt
   practices—United States—History. | Election law—United States.
   | Race discrimination—Political aspects—United States. | United
   States—Politics and government.
Classification: LCC JK1846 .V65 2020 | DDC 324.60973—dc23

LC record available at https://lccn.loc.gov/2020006563

For my advisor, Eric Foner, who has,
by example, modeled the urgency for historians
to respond to the headlines.

Contents

Acknowledgments   ix

Introduction   1

Roundtable   15

Top Ten Articles   91

- Voter Suppression, Then and Now,
  by David W. Blight   93

- How Prisons Change the Balance of Power in America,
  by Heather Ann Thompson   97

- Why We Still Need the Voting Rights Act,
  by John Lewis   106

- Why the Voting Rights Act Is Once Again under Threat,
  by Ari Berman   109

- The Long and Despicable Roots of Voter Suppression
  and Similar Tactics,
  by Frank Palmeri and Ted Wendelin   113

- The Republican Approach to Voter Fraud: Lie,
  by Carol Anderson   119

- How Voter Suppression Could Swing the Midterms,
  by Ari Berman   126

- Stacey Abrams, Brian Kemp, and Neo–Jim Crow
  in Georgia,
  by Carol Anderson   131

- We Cannot Resign Ourselves to Dismay and
  Disenfranchisement,
  by Stacey Abrams   134

- Statement of Stacey Y. Abrams, Founder & Chair,
  Fair Fight Action on Continuing Challenges to the
  Voting Rights Act since *Shelby County v. Holder* before the
  House Judiciary's Subcommittee on the Constitution,
  Civil Rights, and Civil Liberties, June 25, 2019,
  by Stacey Abrams   139

Bibliography   149

Permission Credits   159

Acknowledgments

My first and most important debt is to Deirdre Cooper Owens, the program director at the Library of Company of Philadelphia LCP, who graciously and generously hosted the roundtable at LCP. Special thanks to the staff at LCP, who cheerfully welcomed us, and to Dr. Michael J. Barsanti, who magnanimously supported this endeavor. His commitment to merging civic engagement with historical practice is inspiring, indeed.

While the idea of doing a book on voter suppression felt urgent, my decision to move forward with this project, for better or worse, coincided with the gubernatorial election in Georgia. In the immediate aftermath of the election, Stacey Abrams, the Democratic contender, had exposed evidence of voter suppression. As I sketched the plans for this volume, my History in the Headlines coeditor, Catherine Clinton, suggested Stacey Abrams as a possible contributor. Although I thought it a brilliant idea, I had no idea how I would get in touch with her, until my good friend John Bantivoglio sent out a flurry of e-mails to friends and colleagues in Atlanta. Stacey's enthusiasm to participate in the roundtable and her fierce commitment to democracy are why this book exists. Her insightful and incisive comments during the discussion made this book more than I could have ever hoped. I am also deeply indebted to Samantha Slosberg, who answered countless e-mails and handled logistics on Stacey's behalf.

I am also deeply grateful to the other contributors, who are all leading experts in their own right. Carol Anderson is one of the nation's most prolific and compelling historians on voter suppression. Her intricate knowledge of the law, local history, and politics provided the necessary context for the roundtable—and her effervescence moved us all. Kevin Kruse's commanding understanding of southern political history, his irrepressible wit, and his immediate recognition of the importance of the book were tremendous. Heather Cox Richardson's capacious knowledge of political history and her sophisticated analysis of the Republican Party provided a crucial framework for the discussion. Heather Ann Thompson has been urging historians and the public to recognize the impact of mass incarceration on politics and society for over a decade. Not only did her wholehearted participation in this conversation enrich our understanding of the relationship between prisons and gerrymandering but also her broad knowledge of the twentieth century moved the conversation in productive directions.

I am deeply indebted to Katherine Farr, my undergraduate advisee, who served as a research assistant for this project. She traveled from New London, Connecticut, to Philadelphia to record the roundtable conversation and then spent the summer meticulously and expertly transcribing it. Her brilliant ability to grapple with the nuances of this subject is remarkable. I am also grateful to a few other Connecticut College students—Jackson Bistrong, Dana Gallagher, and Sharon Van Meter—who traveled to Philadelphia to attend the roundtable and supported this endeavor.

Dr. Katherine Kuehler Walters did extensive research on voter suppression and provided key articles that formed the context for the roundtable and the bibliography.

Monica R. Gisolfi and Anne Kornhauser helped me think through the questions for this roundtable, offered excellent historical insights, and provided invaluable feedback and criticism for the introduction.

Many thanks to Catherine Clinton. Although she did not serve as the official editor on this volume, her boundless support, inimitable editorial expertise, and encyclopedic knowledge of southern history and historiography have shaped this volume in more ways than I know or wish to tally.

Mick Gusinde-Duffy, my editor at UGA Press, has championed this series from the start and has been a most excellent and supportive editor from the mere conception of this volume to its completion. This book would not be possible without his alacrity and editorial sophistication. Thank you!

Jim Downs
New York, N.Y.
December 2019

Voter Suppression in U.S. Elections

Introduction

Recently, voter suppression has returned to the headlines. Not since the civil rights movement, over a half century ago, has the national spotlight been so focused on the South for voting discrimination.

On June 25, 2013, the Supreme Court eliminated protections that the Voting Rights Act of 1965 passed to prohibit racial discrimination in voting. The federal government established the Voting Rights Act in 1965 to help guarantee that black people in the South could vote, a right won in the immediate aftermath of the Civil War. The war had ended slavery, with the passage of what became known as the Reconstruction amendments: the Thirteenth Amendment abolished slavery; the Fourteenth Amendment defined formerly enslaved people as citizens; and the Fifteenth Amendment gave black men the right to vote. From the ratification of the Fifteenth Amendment in 1870 to the present, black people's voting rights were only protected when the federal government intervened.

Consequently, the history of voter suppression is a story about the ebbs and flows of the federal government's intervention in the South. Historically, only federal oversight determined fair voting practices in the South. In the immediate aftermath of the Civil War, black people defined freedom by being able to choose their employment, but former slaveholders demanded black people return to the plantation South and reconstitute the agricultural labor force.[1] In response to white southerners' unwillingness to accept emancipation, the federal government created, through the Department of War, a brand-new agency known as the Freedmen's Bureau, to rebuild the South. The Freedmen's Bureau sent federal agents to the South to settle disputes and to negotiate contracts between formerly enslaved people and southern planters. The bureau also responded to other unexpected problems that arose from the transition from slavery to freedom by creating educational, medical, and legal divisions. Since the bureau grew out of the War Department, many of the bureau agents were military officials and thereby had the support of the army to enforce the federal government's new policies.[2]

The bureau, nonetheless, was intended as a temporary institution, as the federal government planned to shift its authority to newly created local and state governments as the South was rebuilt. Thus, the bureau began to shutter its offices by 1869 while the Fifteenth Amendment was being ratified. The Reconstruction amendments were designed to guarantee the creation of a new social order that would make the bureau and even the presence of the U.S. Army in the South obsolete. And it worked. Black people began to vote in record numbers and were elected to serve at all levels of government, from school boards and local law enforcement agencies to the U.S. Congress and state assemblies.

But as soon as military and federal officials began leaving the South in the early 1870s, white southerners began to terrorize black

---

1   Eric Foner, *Reconstruction: America's Unfinished Revolution, 1863–1877* (New York: Harper Perennial, 1988).

2   Foner, *Reconstruction*; Downs, *Sick from Freedom: African American Illness and Suffering during the Civil War and Reconstruction* (New York: Oxford University Press, 2012).

people and intimidate them from voting. Former Confederate soldiers founded the Ku Klux Klan, the racist vigilante group that violently attacked black people, particularly targeting those who had gained political and economic prominence in their communities. Learning about these assaults on black people and on their rights to vote, the federal government once again stepped in and passed the enforcement acts. The first act, passed in 1870, prohibited people from forming groups and masquerading behind disguises to prevent people from voting. A year later, in 1871, the second act removed the power of state governments, based on their malfeasance, to hold elections and placed federal judges and U.S. marshals in charge of those elections. The third act empowered the president to call on armed forces to protect black people from harm when they attempted to vote.[3]

Despite their intent, the enforcement acts failed to protect black voters against the constant threats, terror, and violence that white people waged against them throughout the South. In 1875, just a few years after passage of the enforcement acts, violence escalated in Mississippi. The Democratic Party attempted to overthrow the domination of the Republican Party, which had been the champion of black suffrage since the Civil War. White Democrats organized paramilitary groups called "rifle clubs" that showed up at Republican rallies and violently attacked black voters. On election day, they intimidated black voters by whipping those who attempted to vote and even shooting them. This practice of intimidation

3   "Landmark Legislation: The Enforcement Acts of 1870 and 1871," U.S. Senate, https://www.senate.gov/artandhistory/history/common/generic /EnforcementActs.htm; Hannah Rosen, *Terror in the Heart of Freedom: Citizenship, Sexual Violence, and the Meaning of Race in the Postemancipation South* (Chapel Hill: University of North Carolina Press, 2009).

became known as the Mississippi Plan, which many other states adopted.[4]

Even though the U.S. Army still occupied parts of the South during Reconstruction, the number of troops had decreased. Meanwhile, the federal government and many of the people in power had become frustrated with the amount of money and resources being expended to rebuild the South and wanted to allocate federal support to other problems. The Panic of 1873, a national economic downturn that greatly affected those living in the North and the West, exacerbated such feelings, and many northerners argued that federal money should be used instead to address this crisis. While financial concerns plagued the country, the 1876 presidential election became the unexpected catalyst for the formal evacuation of the army from the South. With the election hinging on returns from the southern states, southern officials promised not to block the election of Rutherford B. Hayes if he promised to withdraw federal troops. This informal agreement became known as the Compromise of 1877, and it, along with a national railroad strike, shifted federal concerns from problems in the South to economic conditions in the entire country—leaving black voters without protection from white southerners committed to restricting their right to vote.[5]

---

4   Steven Hahn, *A Nation under Our Feet: Black Political Struggles in the Rural South from Slavery to the Great Migration* (Cambridge: Harvard University Press, 2005), 288; Vernon Burton, "Race and Reconstruction: Edgefield County, South Carolina," *Journal of Social History* 12, no. 1 (Fall 1978): 31.

5   On the ending of Reconstruction, see Eric Foner, *Reconstruction*. On northern Republicans' abandoning of Reconstruction, see Heather Cox Richardson, *The Death of Reconstruction: Race, Labor, and Politics in the Post–Civil War North, 1865–1901* (Cambridge: Harvard University Press, 2001).

By the 1880s, a new generation of white southerners had emerged, emboldened to restore power to white people.[6] They ignored the Reconstruction amendments and became more aggressive and violent in their efforts to gain power. They slowly but assertively disenfranchised black people from voting by taking control of local and state governments throughout the South. Then, they passed new legislation that disenfranchised black people. They instituted literacy tests and understanding clauses that required people to read arcane, confusing legal jargon. If black voters failed to answer questions posed by white officials about the content of the material, they were denied the right to vote. White southerners also passed poll taxes, which required people to pay a voter registration fee, which also prevented poor people, namely black people, from voting. In addition, state governments mandated that voters show proof of property ownership to be able to cast a ballot, another impossibility for many black people during this period, when so many of them were sharecroppers. Although property requirements, poll taxes, and literacy tests theoretically banned poor white people from voting as well, state governments circumvented such restrictions by passing grandfather clauses, which exempted people, namely white people, whose grandfathers had voted before 1866.[7]

Without the opportunity to vote, black people lost representation in the legislation process and could not serve on juries. These

6   C. Vann Woodward, *Origins of the New South, 1877–1913* (Baton Rouge: Louisiana State University Press, 1951).

7   Michael Perman, *Struggle for Mastery: Disfranchisement in the South* (Chapel Hill: University of North Carolina Press, 2001); J. Morgan Kousser, *Shaping of Southern Politics: Suffrage Restriction and the Establishment of the One Party South* (New Haven: Yale University Press, 1974).

violations of constitutional law combined with the rise of Jim Crow segregation only further restricted black people's access to political power and the application of the Reconstruction amendments. There was, however, some hope in this period of darkness. In some parts of the South, black people, particularly black women, remained committed to creating political change. In North Carolina, for example, Charlotte Hawkins Brown emerged as a key figure who attempted to bridge the schism between white and black people.[8] In other parts of the South, in Louisiana, the Carolinas, and Virginia, black people continued to vote and were elected into state government offices, despite intimidation and violence, from Reconstruction to 1901.[9]

By the beginning of the twentieth century, white southerners, however, had gained control over most of the South. Violence increased, lynchings became more commonplace, and the rise of segregation prevented black people from exercising or gaining political and economic power. The start of World War I, however, unexpectedly offered a way to escape the South. Federal restrictions on immigration, fueled by xenophobic paranoia caused by the war, left the booming manufacturing industries in the North and Midwest without enough employees. Labor agents, in turn, traveled to the South to recruit black men to fill the jobs left vacant in factories, offering them the promise of a better life and a safer community. Between World War I and World War II, millions

8   Glenda Elizabeth Gilmore, *Gender and Jim Crow: Women and the Politics of White Supremacy in North Carolina, 1896–1920* (Chapel Hill: University of North Carolina Press, 1996); Eric Anderson, *Race and Politics in North Carolina, 1872–1901: The Black Second* (Baton Rouge: Louisiana State University Press, 1980).

9   C. Vann Woodward, *The Strange Career of Jim Crow* (New York: Oxford University Press, 1955), 52–55.

of black southerners moved from the South to Chicago, New York, and Philadelphia. This "Great Migration" continued until the 1970s and invariably shifted the black population from the South to other parts of the country, which dramatically altered the South's demographic and the political composition.[10]

Despite the increasing the number of black people fleeing the South, a revolution began to brew. A new generation refused to accept that they could not vote in the South. Black men returning from service as soldiers in World War II refused to accept their status as second-class citizens. Black women, who had suffered sexual violence and assault at the sadistic hands of white men, clandestinely organized political associations and planned boycotts.[11] Slowly but assuredly, black people throughout the South launched campaigns against segregation in schools and public accommodations and fought for the right to vote. They pushed the U.S. government to restore voting rights by registering voters and marching in the streets to demand justice. White students coming of age in other parts of the country learned about the longstanding injustices in the South and vowed to create change. These many efforts evolved into the civil rights movement, a movement that was broad and far-reaching, had many impulses and instigators, and infused

10 James Gregory, *The Southern Diaspora: How the Great Migrations of Black and White Southerners Transformed America* (Chapel Hill: University of North Carolina Press, 2005); James R. Grossman, *Land of Hope: Chicago, Black Southerners, and the Great Migration* (Chicago: University of Chicago Press, 1989); Joe William Trotter Jr., *The Great Migration in Historical Perspective: New Dimensions of Race, Class, and Gender* (Bloomington: Indiana University Press, 1991).

11 Danielle McGuire, *At the Dark End of the Street: Black Women, Rape, and Resistance—a New History of the Civil Rights Movement from Rosa Parks to the Rise of Black Power* (New York: Knopf, 2010).

a sense of justice and rights that ultimately gained the attention of the federal government. Presidents John F. Kennedy and Lyndon B. Johnson, the Supreme Court, and Congress could no longer remain blind to the violations to the Constitution in the South and were forced to take action. Through landmark court cases, federal policy, and federal legislation, the government restored teeth to the Fourteenth and Fifteenth Amendments. Most notably, the government passed the Voting Rights Act, which protected black people's rights to vote by outlawing many discriminatory laws, including literacy tests.[12]

For years, long after the civil rights movement ended, the federal government kept in place protections to guarantee that black people

12 The history of civil rights is vast. On place, see William H. Chafe, *Civilities and Civil Rights: Greensboro, North Carolina, and the Black Struggle for Freedom* (New York: Oxford University Press, 1981); John Dittmer, *Local People: The Struggle for Civil Rights in Mississippi* (Champaign: University of Illinois Press, 1995); Françoise N. Hamlin, *Crossroads at Clarksdale: The Black Freedom Struggle in the Mississippi Delta after World War I* (Chapel Hill: University of North Carolina Press, 2012); and William Sturkey, *Hattiesburg: An American City in Black and White* (Cambridge: Harvard University Press, 2019). On people, see Barbara Ransby, *Ella Baker and the Black Freedom Movement: A Radical Democratic Vision* (Chapel Hill: University of North Carolina, 1998); Katherine Mellen Charron, *Freedom's Teacher: The Life of Septima Clark* (Chapel Hill: University of North Carolina Press, 2009); and Taylor Branch, *At Canaan's Edge: America in the King Years, 1965–68* (New York: Simon & Schuster, 2007). On origins, see Steven F. Lawson and Charles Payne, *Debating the Civil Rights Movement, 1945–1968* (New York: Rowman & Littlefield, 1998); Jacquelyn Dowd Hall, "The Long Civil Rights Movement and the Political Uses of the Past," *Journal of American History* 91, no. 4 (2005); and Glenda Elizabeth Gilmore, *Defying Dixie: The Radical Roots of Civil Rights, 1919–1950* (New York: Norton, 2008). On gender, see McGuire, *At the Dark End of the Street*; and Bettye Collier-Thomas and V. P. Franklin, *Sisters in the Struggle: African-American Women in the Civil Rights–Black Power Movement* (New York: NYU Press, 2001).

could safely participate in democracy and vote. In fact, as congressman and civil rights activist John Lewis explained in 2006, Congress "held 21 hearings, heard from more than 90 witnesses and reviewed more than 15,000 pages of evidence" and determined that the Voting Rights Bill remained necessary due to the threats of discrimination."[13]

All that changed in 2013. Shelby County, which is part of the Alabama jurisdiction, sued the U.S. attorney general Eric H. Holder Jr. claiming that sections of the Voting Rights Bill were unconstitutional. The Voting Rights Act required states that had both a history and contemporary record of voting discrimination to get federal approval before changing their voting regulations. The Supreme Court decided in favor of abandoning such protections. Chief Justice John Roberts, who wrote the majority opinion, claimed this requirement was both outdated and in conflict with state sovereignty. In his opinion, he explained, "Coverage today is based on decades-old data and eradicated practices. The formula captures States by reference to literacy tests and low voter registration and turnout in the 1960s and early 1970s. But such tests have been banned for over 40 years. And voter registration and turnout numbers in covered States have risen dramatically."[14] Justice Ruth Bader Ginsburg, in her dissenting opinion, however, pointed out that such attempts to discriminate had hardly disappeared—in fact, she countered, the Department of Justice had rejected more than seven hundred proposed changes to voting regulations between 1982 and 2006 because they were discriminatory.[15]

---

13 John Lewis, "Why We Still Need the Voting Rights Act," *Washington Post*, February 24, 2013.

14 Shelby County, Alabama v. Holder, attorney general, et al., no. 12-96, argued February 27, 2013—decided June 25, 2013, 18.

15 "The Supreme Court Guts the Voter Rights Act . . . Since Racism Is Over," *The Guardian*, June 25, 2013.

Without the need to get federal approval to change voting practices, state governments have created new ways to suppress the votes of black people. For example, governments have closed nearly three thousand voting poll centers between 2012 and 2016 and have concurrently shut down voting registration drives in predominately black areas.[16] They have cut the number of days allowed for early voting. They have purged voters from registration rolls, claiming residents have moved when, in fact, they have not. They have also removed voters from rolls by claiming that they are inactive and have not voted in a long while based on fallible calculations and problematic databases. And they have required specific forms of identification to vote, such as state's driver's licenses, while closing the offices where such IDs are available. Alabama, for instance, where voter suppression has run rampant, has shuttered thirty-one driver's license offices.[17]

In the Alabama case, the NAACP filed a federal lawsuit (*Greater Birmingham Ministries v. Alabama*) against Alabama's requirement to have a driver's license to vote and cited the example of an eighteen-year-old high school student who could not vote in 2016 because she did not have a license. While she could qualify for a state-issued ID to vote, the closest DMV was forty miles from her home and no form of public transportation was available for her to get to it.[18]

16 "Seven Ways Alabama Has Made it Harder to Vote," *New York Times*, June 23, 2018.

17 Ibid. Also on the problems with driver's licenses but in Mississippi, see "Proposal Would Make Mississippi Voter ID Stricter," *AP NEWS*, February 2, 2019.

18 "LDF Files Lawsuit to Challenge Alabama's Racially Discriminatory Photo ID Law," LDF, December 2, 2015, https://www.naacpldf.org/update/ldf-files -lawsuit-challenge-alabamas-racially-discriminatory-photo-id-law/.

State governments have also invalidated other government-issued forms of ID, like federal public-housing IDs, in favor of driver's licenses. In addition, they have passed laws requiring a person's name to appear exactly the same on a driver's license as it does on the voter rolls. If a discrepancy occurs, no matter how slight—an initial instead of a middle name, a missing hyphen—that person cannot vote. A few weeks before the governor's race in Georgia between Democrat Stacey Abrams and Republican secretary of state Brian Kemp, for instance, the state, under authority of the office that Kemp himself was in charge of, put on hold more than fifty-three thousand potential voters because of such so-called mismatches.[19]

Because of the South has a legacy of restricting black people from voting that dates back to the end of the Civil War, this book, as part of the History in the Headlines series, aims to place voter suppression today into the broader historical context by bringing together leading experts on the subject. We believe that history can provide analysis to help end this crisis. When isolated, individual cases of voter suppression—an unmatched name on a voter roll or a closed polling site—may seem incidental or even accidental, but placed within a broader chronology, these actions become part of a much longer, deeply entrenched system of oppression that dates back to the nineteenth century.

19 "Georgia's 'Exact Match' Law Could Potentially Harm Many Eligible Voters," *Washington Post*, October 20, 2018; "GOP Candidate Improperly Purged 340,000 from Georgia Voter Rolls, Investigation Claims," *The Guardian*, October 19, 2018; "Block the Vote: A Journalist Discusses Voting Rights and Restrictions," Fresh Air, NPR, August 10, 2015; Carol Anderson, *One Person, No Vote: How Voter Suppression Is Destroying Our Democracy* (New York: Bloomsbury, 2018); Ari Berman, *Give Us the Ballot: The Modern Struggle for Voting Rights in America* (New York: Farrar, Straus and Giroux, 2015).

The History in the Headlines series aspires to provide historical analysis of current events to a broad audience. Often, scholarly insights and ideas on such subjects are found across a broad spectrum of books and articles; this series brings these voices together in a single place. Each book consists of an actual conversation among leading experts about a particular subject, articles pertaining to the subject, and a bibliography of related sources and further reading. The conversation among experts is recorded, transcribed, and edited for clarity. The objective is to capture the interplay among prominent thinkers as they grapple with a particular problem.

This volume's conversation includes the input of five truly dynamic and brilliant contributors. A Yale Law School Alumnus, Stacey Abrams was the Democratic nominee in the 2018 governor's race in Georgia. Due to Georgia's harrowed history of voter suppression, she has become a leading advocate for voter rights. She draws on her personal experience during the 2018 race as well as her impeccable knowledge of the law to contribute to the discussion. Carol Anderson, a best-selling and award-winning historian, wrote one of the most important books on voter suppression, *One Person, No Vote*. Based on her research on how voter suppression affects African Americans and other minorities, Anderson offers compelling evidence of the policies and practices that have defined voter suppression in the last few decades. Kevin Kruse adds his commanding knowledge of the history of the twentieth-century South to help frame the conversation. As an expert in nineteenth-century political history, Heather Cox Richardson expands the parameters of the conversation by offering incisive detail about political parties in the 1800s and their attitudes about voting and citizenship. Heather Ann Thompson, who won both the Pulitzer and Bancroft Prizes for *Blood in the Water: The Attica Prison Uprising of 1971 and*

Its Legacy, deftly places the subject of voter suppression within the context of mass incarceration and gerrymandering. The conversation was moderated by Jim Downs, coeditor of the History in the Headlines series.

As with other volumes in the series, to provide context for the conversation this volume includes reprints of ten important articles that appeared in newspapers and magazines on the subject at hand. Between 2013 to 2019, newspaper editorials often alerted the public to the problems caused by voting suppression and generated debate and discussion throughout the United States and beyond. These articles chronicling the current crisis surrounding voter suppression include Pulitzer Prize–winning historian David Blight's *New York Times* 2012 op-ed on voter suppression in the present and the past; legendary civil rights activist and congressman John Lewis's 2013 editorial in *The Washington Post*, published during the week when the Supreme Court heard *Shelby County v. Holder*; incisive editorials by two of the conversation contributors, Stacey Abrams and Carol Anderson; and compelling editorials by leading journalist Ari Berman. The section also includes deeper dives into voter suppression: Heather Ann Thompson, one of the conversation contributors, offers an insightful analysis of the relationship between voter suppression and mass incarceration, while Frank Palmeri and Ted Wendelin provide a rich historical overview of voter suppression. Due to the unique fortune of having Stacey Abrams as a contributor to the book's conversation, we also added the important testimony she delivered before the House Judiciary's Subcommittee on the Constitution to this section.

Since black people were first given the right to vote in the nineteenth century, there have been people committed to taking their rights away. The federal government has over the course of both the nineteenth and twentieth centuries enacted political and legal measures to safeguard black people's right, but over time those protections have either been denied or dismantled. This book hopes to end that pattern by offering historical analysis so that voter suppression no longer appears in the headlines.

Roundtable
on Voter Suppression
in U.S. Elections

April 5, 2019   *Library Company of Philadelphia*

MODERATOR

Jim Downs is professor of history at Connecticut College, where he is also the director of the American studies program. He earned his BA from the University of Pennsylvania and his MA and PhD from Columbia. He is the author of *Sick from Freedom: African American Illness and Suffering during the Civil War and Reconstruction* and *Stand By Me: The Forgotten History of Gay Liberation*. He has coedited four other academic anthologies and has published articles in *The Atlantic*, *Time* magazine, the *New York Times*, the *New Republic*, *Slate*, and *Vice*, among others. He is the coeditor of the History in the Headlines series.

PANELISTS

Stacey Abrams is a *New York Times* best-selling author, serial entrepreneur, nonprofit CEO, and political leader. After serving for eleven years in the Georgia House of Representatives, seven as minority leader, in 2018, Abrams became the Democratic nominee for governor of Georgia, when she won more votes than any other Democrat in the state's history. Abrams was the first black woman to become the gubernatorial nominee for a major party in the United States. After witnessing the gross mismanagement of the 2018 election by the secretary of state's office, Abrams launched Fair Fight to ensure every Georgian has a voice in our election system. Over the course of her career, Abrams has founded multiple organizations devoted to voting rights, training and hiring young people of color, and tackling social issues at both the state and national levels including Fair Count—to ensure that the 2020 Census is fair, accurate, and complete. Abrams received degrees from Spelman College, the LBJ School of Public Affairs at the University of Texas, and Yale Law School. She and her five siblings grew up in Gulfport, Mississippi, and Georgia.

Carol Anderson is the Charles Howard Candler Professor and Chair of African American Studies at Emory University and a Guggenheim Fellow in Constitutional Studies. She is the author of several books, including *Eyes off the Prize: The United Nations and the African-American Struggle for Human Rights, 1944–1955*, which was published by Cambridge University Press and awarded both the Gustavus Myers and Myrna Bernath Book Awards; *White Rage: The Unspoken Truth of Our Racial Divide*, which won the 2016 National Book Critics Circle Award for Criticism and was also a *New York Times* best seller and a *New York Times* Editor's Pick. Her most recent book, *One Person, No Vote: How Voter Suppression Is Destroying Our Democracy*, was long-listed for the National Book Award in Nonfiction and was a finalist for the PEN/Galbraith Book Award in Nonfiction.

Kevin M. Kruse specializes in twentieth-century American political history, with special attention to conflicts over race, religion, and rights. He received his undergraduate degree from the University of North Carolina at Chapel Hill and his MA and PhD degrees from Cornell University. He is a professor of history at Princeton University, where he has served on the faculty since 2000. Kruse is the author of *White Flight: Atlanta and the Making of Modern Conservatism*, *One Nation Under God: How Corporate America Invented Christian America*, and, with Julian Zelizer, *Fault Lines: A History of the United States since 1974*, as well as the coeditor of three essay collections. He is currently working on his next project, titled "The Division: John Doar, the Justice Department, and the Civil Rights Movement."

Heather Cox Richardson is professor of history at Boston College and the author of a number of books about American politics, including *To Make Men Free: A History of the Republican Party* and most recently *How the South Won the Civil War: Oligarchy, Democracy, and the Continuing Fight for the Soul of America*. She writes widely for popular publications and is a national commentator on American political history and the Republican Party. Her work has appeared in *The Guardian*, the *Washington Post*, the *New York Times*, the *Chicago Tribune*, and *Quartz*, among other publications, and she is the author of "Letters from an American," an online chronicle of the U.S. government.

Heather Ann Thompson is a native Detroiter and historian on faculty of the University of Michigan in Ann Arbor in the departments of history and Afro-American and African studies and at the Residential College. Her recent book, *Blood in the Water: The Attica Prison Uprising of 1971 and Its Legacy*, profiled on television and radio programs across the country, won the Pulitzer Prize in History, the Bancroft Prize in American History and Diplomacy, the Ridenhour Book Prize, the J. Willard Hurst Prize, and a New York City Bar Association book prize. The book was also named a finalist for the National Book Award, the Los Angeles Book Prize in History, and the Silver Gavel Award from the American Bar Association, and it was named on fourteen best books of 2016 lists including those compiled by the *New York Times*, *Newsweek*, *Kirkus Reviews*, the *Boston Globe*, *Publishers Weekly*, *Bloomberg*, the *Marshall Project*, the *Baltimore City Paper*, *Book Scroll*, and the *Christian Science Monitor*. Additionally, *Blood in the Water* appeared on the Best Human Rights Books of 2016 list and received starred reviews from *Library Journal*, *Kirkus*, and *Publishers Weekly*. *Blood in the Water* has also been optioned by TriStar Pictures and will be adapted for film by acclaimed screenwriters Anna Waterhouse and Joe Schrapnel.

DOWNS: I am going to ask the panelists to start with an icebreaker. Tell a story about the first time you voted, or your earliest voting memory, or possibly your favorite vote, or your most monumental vote, and then we'll move into the questions. So who would like to start?

[The participants all look at Anderson]

KRUSE: [To Anderson] *One Person, One Vote*, right?

[Laughter]

ANDERSON: It's hard for me . . . so I can think more of a political memory.

DOWNS: Right.

ANDERSON: And there are just these series of snapshots that happened. There was the assassination of JFK, and I remember the women in church crying, and I remember it being this incredible moment because you knew something had shifted in the universe. I remember feeling ill at ease as Nixon came to power, and I'm still a child but something didn't quite feel right. So as a kid I'm on the front porch reading all of the books that I can on Watergate and glued to the Watergate hearings because I was watching democracy in action, and so I knew then, just as I knew when King was killed and when RFK was assassinated, that the power to vote and what is happening in our political processes really shape our world and that it is absolutely essential to be involved. And as I became a historian, I began to realize how much African Americans had been pulled out of full engagement in terms of shaping our world through the political process, and I was determined that that wasn't going to happen again.

DOWNS: That's powerful, great. Heather, Kevin, anyone?

RICHARDSON: Well, it's funny you say that because I remember Watergate in a huge way. I was quite young during that, but for me my big voting memory was not voting. Nineteen eighty when Ronald Reagan ran, I thought, "No way. Who's going to elect an actor who clearly has no grasp of anything and who is making stuff up?" So I didn't vote because he was going to lose and he was going down in flames. And it was a warm night—I was in college, it was my first semester of college. And I remember just sitting on the edge of a desk—and the window was open—and listening to people on campus celebrating, and thinking, "I need to understand this, I need to understand how this happened."

[Murmurs of approval]

RICHARDSON: Because the relationship between the image this man projected and the reality that he was going to deliver was going to hit everybody really hard. And it was really . . . You know, I was actually studying folklore and mythology at the time—I wasn't in history—but I was like, "This is a change moment." And do you know, I have never missed an election since. Local elections, sick, new baby, whatever, I am out there voting because it's never going to happen again that I don't speak up.

ANDERSON: Yeah, yeah.

ABRAMS: So for me there are two. When we were growing up, my mom and dad—usually my mom because she would take us when she picked us all up—they would take us with them to vote. I'm the second of six children, and there's twelve years between the oldest and youngest, so we looked like *Make Way for Ducklings*.

[Laughter]

ABRAMS: But she intentionally would always take us with her to vote, and my dad, if he got off work, he would go with us at the same time because he would always vote as well, but Mom was the one who had the car. So I just remember us sort of trailing out of the voting booth because we couldn't all fit inside, but she wanted us to see her in the act of voting.

ANDERSON: Ah.

ABRAMS: And then the only fight I ever got into in school, the only actual physical altercation, was around the 1980 election. A classmate and I vehemently disagreed about Reagan versus Carter, and she called Carter a communist, and I told her, "You don't say things like that about him," and I told her that Reagan was just an actor—it was an epithet to me. She threw a book at me, and I shoved my desk at her.

[Laughter]

ABRAMS: We were both told to back off and sit down, but yes, I got into my first fight Democrat versus Republican in second grade.

KRUSE: Impressive.

ABRAMS: I won.

[More laughter]

KRUSE: I don't have a story anywhere near as good as those. My first voting memory was a preschool mock election in 1976 in which I voted for Jerry Ford because, well, I knew Ford played golf and my dad played golf too.

[Laughter]

KRUSE: That was about the depth of the engagement. My favorite votes, though, were when I lived in Atlanta when I was writing my dissertation on Atlanta, I got to vote for John Lewis as my congressman which was *great*. I'd never had congressmen I was really excited about before, but that was a cool one to pull the lever for—a civil rights icon who'd literally bled for voting rights. And beyond that moment, I've done the same thing with my kids that your mom and your dad did with you. I remember I wheeled in my daughter in her stroller at 6:15 in the morning to vote for Obama in 2008, and ever since then we've taken them into the booth with us, closed the curtain, and really just stressed how important it is.

ANDERSON: Yeah.

KRUSE: Because I feel it's as much of an important ritual civically as going to church is for me religiously. I mean it really is—it's a serious and important moment. And like church, it can't be an irregular thing. State and local elections, primaries and generals, it's all important. And I wanted to instill that value in them.

THOMPSON: Because I grew up with parents who were pretty dubious about electoral politics (they had, for example, protested both Democrats and Republicans over the issue of the Vietnam War), I am not sure I fully "got" how much difference an election could make until I was a senior in high school—1980. I attended an all-black high school in the city of Detroit, and I will never forget the day after Reagan was elected. It was silent in the school. The students were in mourning. They knew—in their gut they knew—that this was a election after which all would get much worse for people who lived in cities like ours. I will never forget that day. From then on, as soon as I was old enough to cast my ballot, I did.

DOWNS: Wow! Okay, so let's shift to the discussion. How can history be used as a way to help illuminate the crisis surrounding voter suppression? So if we look at isolated cases of voter suppression, you could just say that's an aberration, right? But when you place it within a broader historical context, it becomes part of a larger chronology of oppression. If you look at isolated problems at a voting poll, they might be seen as incidental or even accidental, but when you place it within the broader context of history, it appears criminal. So I really want to see what we can do here today as historians and as politicians, as activists, as thinkers, in terms of how we could use history as a way to elucidate this larger crisis. So my first priority would be to clarify the terms in order to orient the reader. So how would you define voter suppression?

RICHARDSON: Don't we have to defer to Carol on this one? [Laughter]

ANDERSON: No, no! We're all in this!

DOWNS: Yes!

ANDERSON: I mean, voter suppression is . . . are those policies that are systematically put in place that are targeted toward key segments of the voting population to ensure that either they don't vote, can't vote, or that you're increasing the degree of difficulty for them to be able to cast their vote.

DOWNS: Right.

ANDERSON: And when we begin to understand what that looks like, that's why history is so important, and so I'm just going to kind of roll for a minute. So when I started working on *One Person, No Vote*, I started historically because I wanted to tell the story about the 2016 election, but I couldn't tell that story about the 2016 election without going back to the Mississippi Plan of 1890.

DOWNS: Right.

ANDERSON: Because that Mississippi Plan of 1890 is when the Mississippi state legislature said, "How do we stop black folk from voting? But we've got this Fifteenth Amendment that says 'the state shall not abridge the right to vote on account of race, color, or previous condition of servitude.' How do you stop black folk from voting without writing a law saying we don't want black people to vote?" And so what Mississippi did was to create an array of policies that looked at the societally imposed conditions that were imposed on African Americans and then used those conditions as the litmus test for access into the ballot.

DOWNS: Right.

ANDERSON: And when you look now at Jim Crow 2.0, with the voter suppression we have now, it's the same thing.

KEVIN KRUSE: Uh huh.

[Murmurs of approval]

ANDERSON: You close polls, then you're dealing with issues of distance and the lack of public transportation for people to be able to get to the polls. You have massive disparities in poverty, and so you use things like requiring an ID that people don't have, because you're defining what types of IDs.

DOWNS: Right.

ANDERSON: And so history allows us to see the context and also to see, I mean it's the way they said . . . you know, it wasn't just the literacy test; it wasn't just the poll tax; it wasn't just the grandfather clause. They knew that by having an array. If they couldn't catch you this way, they'd get you this way; if they couldn't catch you, oh, they'd get you this way; if they couldn't do it, they'd get you this way. And so by having to jump over all of these obstacles, it therefore made it doubly difficult for African Americans to be able to vote, and that's what we're seeing today.

STACEY ABRAMS: The only piece I would add is the taxonomy that we use in the political space is to say it's "registration access, ballot access, and ballot counting." That it's "Can you register? If you can register, can you stay registered?"

[Murmurs of approval]

ABRAMS: "If you are removed from the rolls, can you get back on the rolls?" Then, ballot access: "Can you get to your polling place? Did your polling location close? Did it move? Is there a guard? . . . Is there a sheriff standing outside, whose very presence discourages you from going inside?" What we saw happening in Hancock County in Georgia when too many black people voted in an election, the state legislator, who is also the county attorney, worked with the secretary of state to authorize sheriff's deputies to follow black men home to inquire as to their legitimacy as electors, but in a state where we have the highest number of people on probation or parole, the very act of asking the question served to disadvantage them from thinking they should have the right to vote.

RICHARDSON: Yeah.

ABRAMS: So, ballot access is also "Can you get your absentee ballot when you apply for it? Can you trust the system that says that . . . you know, the check is in the mail, that the ballot is in the mail? Can you . . . do you have a database that adequately and accurately reflects who you are?" One of the challenges for Georgia, of course, is that . . . and . . . I know this is true in Florida and other states because each county individually maintains a database that is either delivered by or overseen by the secretary of state. There is no quality control for the database. Therefore, you may or may not know that you have access to the ballot until you show up to actually cast your ballot, even though you have your card and you checked the website. But when you get there, because of the poll log, you may or may not show up as registered and be allowed to cast a ballot. Then the third issue is ballot counting, which I just refer to as "Florida."

[Laughter]

ABRAMS: That is the issue if you cast a ballot: Would it actually count? Also, it is the signature match requirement that is particularly pervasive. It's the fact that in states where you move a polling place, it affects the voter. Even though everyone is entitled to take time off to vote, not every state allows you to be paid for that time off, which means, if you must lose pay to travel to another polling place, there is a poll tax. If you get to a precinct only to find that it's been closed or it's underresourced, you're in line for four hours, which is what happened in our state, that's an actual poll tax. Because you are losing pay—if you're a shift worker that can be up to half a day's pay.

ANDERSON: Mmhmm.

ABRAMS: And your vote does not count simply because you are never allowed to actually cast it. Registration access, ballot access, and ballot counting, and the fact that they discarded ballots for "signature mismatch" on the absentee ballot or for "misinformation," and the rules differ not just from state to state but from county to county.

RICHARDSON: Yeah.

ABRAMS: The fact that you can have a divergent democracy within the same state is deeply problematic; thus when I think of voter suppression, it is each of those individual barriers. But it is the systemic connection that creates not only these hurdles but hobbles you from the very beginning and holds you accountable for your own ability to change the system.

KRUSE: Mmhmm.

ABRAMS: You have no agency to accomplish this, but you have the obligation to do so, and that's where voter suppression is the most pervasive and the most insidious.

DOWNS: So are these individual cases of voter suppression invisible because of this larger history? We often think about history in terms of how it can help elucidate this problem, but I'm wondering how history might be exacerbating the problem of voter suppression by setting up a framework and definition of voter suppression that no longer exists but nonetheless transpires more subversively? How has the history of voting—of very obvious forms of oppression of not letting people vote—unwittingly obscured these contemporary cases, which on the surface don't appear as systematic?

ANDERSON: I think that part of the problem is that when we think of disfranchisement and voter suppression we think of Selma.

KRUSE: Yeah.

ANDERSON: We need to see in this society—I mean this is what I talked about in *White Rage*—we are so focused in on the flames that we miss the kindling.

KRUSE AND RICHARDSON: Uh huh.

ANDERSON: We need to see the dramatic confrontation where people are being blocked from the ballot boxes, are being blocked from being able to vote, that you've got sheriffs lined up—we've got that kind of visual power, that image. And so when voter suppression then moves into the kind of quiet, bureaucratic, what I call that kind of "slow burn" of democracy . . .

DOWNS: Right, right.

ANDERSON: Where it's so mundane that it doesn't attract media attention, but when you think about it, a Brennan Center for Justice report showed that sixteen million people were purged from the voter rolls between 2014 and 2016.

KRUSE: Mmhmm.

ANDERSON: If we saw sixteen million bodies piled up, we would say, "Oh my *God*, something's gone wrong," but we don't see that because this is quiet—it is hidden—and as Stacey Abrams has said, it is one of those things where the onus is put on the individual to uphold the constitutional right to vote, and it's not put on the state to uphold the constitutional right to vote. And so that kind of shift and imbalance then disrupts that narrative that we saw coming out of the civil rights movement. With the civil rights movement, we understood that there were structural inequalities in the United States, but one of the ideological shifts that happened was to then say, "Well, the signs came down."

KRUSE AND ABRAMS: Right.

ANDERSON: So those signs came down, and so now inequality has to be a personal issue. You've got a "personal failing." You have a "culture of poverty." And so to then make these kinds of failings a personal issue then allows the state to abdicate any responsibility for the kinds of voter suppression that it has implemented.

KRUSE: And it's a shift in tactics.

ANDERSON: Yes.

KRUSE: There was an evolution of conservatism that I think is really vitally important to remember here. There had been an important shift in the government's attitude on issues of racial discrimination and segregation from being one in which the government had largely propped *up* those systems to, in the 1960s, the tools of government were now being used to tear those systems *down*. And in response there was a new movement on the right which said effectively, "Hold on, these things are the same." Right? "If the government can't be involved in separating the races, then the government shouldn't be involved in pushing the races together. These are the same thing." And it's the rise of so-called colorblind conservatism.

ANDERSON: Yes.

KRUSE: Pat Buchanan had a line in 1976—the former Nixon aide, not exactly progressive on issues of race—

ANDERSON: Not *exactly* [laughs].

KRUSE: Not exactly, and Buchanan said that if we wanted to end racial conflict in America, then the first step along that road is to make the government of the United States colorblind. It's a distortion of King's line in the March on Washington speech that we shouldn't judge people by the color of their skin but by the content of their character. Conservatives like Buchanan seize on that line, which King meant as a critique of state-sanctioned segregation and discrimination, to assert that the government shouldn't be involved in racial issues in *any* way. That is an incredible misreading, obviously, as everyone in this room knows, of what King said in support of government policies like affirmative action and of course civil rights legislation.

[Chuckling]

KRUSE: But it's a misreading that conservatives seize on all the same. And so what happens out of that? Initially, this color-blind conservatism was focused solely on programs that were designed for racial redress, so affirmative action, solutions to housing segregation, things like that. But over time it came to encompass voting rights too. In 1987 the conservative scholar Abigail Thernstrom had a book titled *Whose Votes Count?* In it, she argued that the Voting Rights Act was essentially a form of affirmative action for the electorate. Right?

DOWNS: Right.

RICHARDSON: Yes.

KRUSE: And this then is a line that gets picked up in conservative legal circles. So when you get to the point where the Supreme Court is discussing *Shelby County v. Holder* in the oral arguments, Justice Scalia asserted that continued support for the Voting Rights Act was a perpetuation of racial entitlement. Scalia says that support for the Voting Rights Act is a perpetuation of racial entitlement.

ANDERSON: Mmhmm.

[Someone in the room exhales sharply.]

KRUSE: So, from this perspective, the Voting Rights Act isn't about equality—it's about giving African Americans an unfair advantage.

ANDERSON: Yes.

KRUSE: Which is a bizarre misreading of history, but it comes from that erasure, right?

ANDERSON: Yes.

KRUSE: That sense that the government needs to fade out of this sphere . . . It shouldn't hurt African Americans any more, but it certainly shouldn't help them either.

RICHARDSON: And that leads directly into the 1993 Motor Voter Act and the response to that, the idea that somehow enabling people to vote is giving privileges to people who at the time were called Democratic voters, because Motor Voter enrollment was going to be possible also in welfare offices.

KRUSE: Mmhmm.

DOWNS: Right.

RICHARDSON: And that is fascinating because it's '93 and that is the same year that [Republican strategist] Ed Rollins goes into the newspapers and says, "You know, I got a GOP governor elected in New Jersey by suppressing the black vote," and then you start to see GOP people increasingly saying, "There's no way that Clinton should have won. There's no way Democrats should win. They're only winning because there are illegitimate voters."

ANDERSON: Yes.

RICHARDSON: So really interestingly, you guys probably don't remember, but there was that period when—it was in '96, I think it was—where Dianne Feinstein and Mary Landrieu, California and Louisiana, both were elected, but the House and the Senate had yearlong investigations, and every night the GOP leaders were on the news saying it was illegitimate . . .

KRUSE: Mmhmm.

RICHARDSON: "This was an illegitimate election. They were illegitimately elected. The voters shouldn't have voted. They're dead people." Whatever.

ANDERSON: Yes.

RICHARDSON: And from that, at the end of the day the report said, "Yeah, they were fairly elected," but I think it's Newt Gingrich goes on TV and says, "Well, the only reason we couldn't find the illegitimate voters is because they hid it so well. We know these elections were illegitimate, but they hid it so well."

ANDERSON: Right, right, right!

KRUSE: Mmhmm.

RICHARDSON: And that's one of the things that bleeds into this idea of illegitimate voters. And then in 1997, that Miami election.

ANDERSON: Oh.

RICHARDSON: Yeah, the mayoral election in Miami when, which was completely corrupt, but that's 1998 then, you wrote about this, 1998, Florida passes the Voter Registration Act that cuts— you had a number in *One Person, No Vote*—like twenty thousand people off the voter rolls?

ANDERSON: Something like that.

RICHARDSON: The U.S. Commission on Civil Rights called it closer to one hundred thousand. The Florida law went into place in 1998, and then we get 2000.

ANDERSON: Right.

RICHARDSON: And it works!

ANDERSON: It works.

RICHARDSON: Voter suppression works, and then you get your sixteen million number.

DOWNS: Heather?

THOMPSON: I was also going to say, to your question of why Americans don't seem to fully appreciate what such a long history of voter suppression has meant—why folks miss something that is so glaringly obvious—is that I think that certainly journalists, but even historians, see low voter turnout and confuse that absence at the polls with apathy. We just assume that when people don't vote, they just didn't care enough to show up. We don't call enough attention to the myriad barriers that have been placed there to stop them from showing up.

[Murmurs of approval]

RICHARDSON: Yeah.

THOMPSON: This seemed particularly how folks understood what happened in 2016. There was so much talk about how white voter turnout's up and black voter turnout's down.

ANDERSON: Right.

KRUSE: Mmhmm.

THOMPSON: And this observation was understood to somehow shine light not just on why the election went the way that it did but also on which Americans really cared about the race and cared about the contenders running. Ironically, the white vote actually was not up very significantly, and though the black vote was down, that was due to these often so-hidden barriers to voting that people literally don't see. I mean, let's be clear: by 2016 there were about 6.1 million African American voters who were literally unable to vote—formally disfranchised—some 25 percent in Kentucky, 27 percent in many southern states, and even some 18 percent in states like Wyoming. And so these are voters that are immediately assumed to be apathetic voters but who literally are forbidden from weighing in when we have an election.

DOWNS: Right.

THOMPSON: Seeing this as apathy has had deadly consequences. In short, those with the ability to vote start to think about those who actually don't, "Well, if you don't care about the franchise, why in the hell should the government aid your ability to cast the ballot or even aid your ability to go to register?"

KRUSE: To circle back to Carol's point, it's the visuals of this. It's not Jim Clark with his billy club on the steps of the Dallas County Courthouse beating women.

THOMPSON: Exactly.

KRUSE: It's a bloodless purge or a purge that—again this is what this colorblind conservatism does, is it applies what ostensibly seems to be a racially neutral language and these kind of ideas mapped over on suburban innocence and all these other things that permeate the discourse, but that "it's not racism here," right?

ANDERSON: Right.

KRUSE: That any kind of felon would be barred . . .

THOMPSON: But also, it's the widely held idea that it's not suppression. It's voluntary. It's voter apathy.

KRUSE: Right, right.

THOMPSON: Because "if you wanted to work hard to get your voting rights back you could."

ABRAMS: Exactly.

KRUSE: Right, well, "anyone can go get a driver's license and vote, right?"

THOMPSON: Anyone.

KRUSE: "Anyone can go do this or that."

ABRAMS: It's also the complicity of the candidates.
Because part of the reason voter suppression works is that we've created this culture that says you don't question the outcome of elections.

MOST OF THE PARTICIPANTS AND ONLOOKERS: Mmmhmm!

ABRAMS: Unless the act is so egregious as to be absolutely clear on its face. The most common response I get to the fact that I refused to concede the election is "Well, Nixon conceded his election in 1960, and aren't you destroying democracy by questioning the election?" Part of the historical challenge is that there aren't a lot of moments where we question the outcome. You don't have to call into question the whole of democracy to say that the process may not have been valid.

KRUSE: Right.

ABRAMS: And the few times we've seen it happen the pile-on . . . We are essentially given a couple of weeks to be angry or worried, but after that you have to get over it. So Al Gore—there's this moment where the shift from being concerned about the integrity of our system becomes "Well, you shouldn't be telling . . . or we shouldn't be challenging this in a public space."

DOWNS AND KRUSE: Right.

ABRAMS: And my response is constantly "I acknowledge the legality, but I refuse to concede the legitimacy."

ANDERSON: Yes.

KRUSE: Uh huh.

ABRAMS: Part of that, I think, calls into necessity urging both the pundits in the press as well as the candidates to recognize that we may not have answers by 11:00 p.m. on the night of the election, that the process isn't made invalid because you question it and make sure that it is proper and correct. But as long as candidates are told that you cannot run again if you question the process, then you create this complicity that becomes not only pervasive but repetitive; and so every election in Florida should be called into question.

[Laughter]

ABRAMS: Elections in Georgia, also elections in Wisconsin, and what happened in North Dakota. There are legitimate questions that could be raised, but the candidates who typically are either the victims or the benefactors are disinclined to say anything because our culture, which I think historians can help us recast, our culture says that asking the question in itself diminishes our democracy.

KRUSE: Well then, there's . . . let me just . . . because you mentioned Nixon. That's actually a myth that Nixon didn't challenge.

ABRAMS: Yeah, I know.

ANDERSON: Right.

KRUSE: And it's a myth that comes out of Nixon's own autobiography *Six Crises*. Nixon was ready to challenge. The RNC launched "field checks" in eight different states to challenge the results on the ground. This idea that he kind of threw up his hands and said, "Well, the voters have spoken and I'll obey that," is total nonsense. But it's used now as you say over and over again to say, "Well, look, if Nixon would accept a contested election, then surely you can too. You're better than Nixon, right?"

ANDERSON: And we can . . . I did a piece that talked about the social construct that we have in the United States of okaying illegitimate regimes. And so I looked at for instance the [Theodore] Bilbo election in '46 in Mississippi. And Bilbo had said . . . he was out there because in '46 black veterans had come back from the war and they were ready for democracy—they were ready to fight for democracy—this is why you get a wave of lynching happening in '46.

[Murmurs of approval]

ANDERSON: Because black folks were like "not today." And so Bilbo is out there really riling up his followers saying, "You know how to stop a Negro from voting? You get a rope and some tar and feathers and you don't forget the matches," right? And so, you get incredible violence happening, as black people are trying to vote.

KRUSE: Right.

ANDERSON: The NAACP and African Americans in Mississippi challenge the results of that election because clearly the Fifteenth Amendment had been violated.

DOWNS: Right.

ANDERSON: And that case went all the way up into Congress, then Congress is like, "Eh, weeell . . . mmmm . . . I mean we really shouldn't . . . I mean really . . ." and so you get this kind of sense that as long as you do the violence, you get to be the winner of the spoils.

DOWNS: Right.

ANDERSON: Regardless of how that was created. And so I'm just going to say right here [to Abrams] when you stood up, *Oh my gosh*.

THOMPSON: Yes.

[Laughter, especially from Anderson]

ANDERSON: Oh, I just felt, "Oh it's a new day." Because I was so tired. I was tired of Bilbo. I was tired of Gore. It was really clear what had happened then, and when you said, "Oh no, not today. I refuse. This is not a concession speech," it's like this is the new narrative that we need if we're going to have the democracy that we truly deserve. You can't cheat. You can't lie. You can't eviscerate American citizens' basic rights.

DOWNS: Right so, [Abrams starts to speak] go ahead.

ABRAMS: The one thing I would say, just to go back to the core question, is this exact conversation of having the actual truth tellers who recorded that history respond in the moment of the miscasting of what has happened, because, you know, I was on *Firing Line* when Margaret Hoover (a PBS show) asked me the questions.

KRUSE: Right.

ABRAMS: I had not read your book, so I didn't know. I responded from my gut, but it is having the capacity of history to correct the record in real time, because we tell the same myths over and over again until they sound like truth.

DOWNS: Right.

KRUSE: Uh huh.

ABRAMS: Where I think historians can help preserve and restore democracy is to remind us of how we got it and what the challenges have been and to contextualize the fact that history repeats itself. And that piece is often forgotten, particularly by those of us who are trying to make the next round of history.

DOWNS: Okay. So that refusal to concede, could you just walk us through how you got there? [The participants chuckle.] Because as a historian I saw it, and it was moving, and I sent it to my students—the *Rolling Stone* clip—and I was like, "This is tight!" But then I was wondering, "When . . . did you figure that out? Did you go for a run that day? Was it over a cup of chai latte with a friend?"

[Laughter]

DOWNS: How did you get that strength? ... How did you develop that stance?

ABRAMS: So I would say it started on the sixth, so by 1:00 a.m. The Associated Press had not called my race, but they had called my friend Andrew Gillum's race [the Florida governor's race the same year], and Andrew had already conceded the race before it was called. I understood exactly what happened to Andrew, that likely he was in a room with a group of consultants and advisers who said, "This is what you need to do, and it's for the good of order; it's for the good of the future." I was in a different room. My dad had gone to jail registering people to vote; my mother had been the first woman to do lots of things; but most of all I had my parents and siblings in the room and my campaign team. We all had been listening and working for the last three weeks, hearing story after story of voter suppression.

ANDERSON: Mmhmm.

ABRAMS: On election day, Chelsey Hall, who was my special assistant, and I had actually traveled from South Georgia up to Atlanta, stopping along the way. We heard story after story of voter suppression. So by the time we get to the hotel that night, there's no legitimacy to the process.

KRUSE: Right.

ABRAMS: My first responsibility was to say that we weren't going to allow the vote to be called until we were certain every vote was counted, and we had ample evidence that wasn't happening. We had already filed two emergency petitions to keep polling places open, and by not conceding on the first day, the goal was to just make certain that every vote counted. Then, during the process over the next ten days, we saw the first sort of a wave, then a trickle, then another wave of new votes that were counted simply because we asked the question. There were four lawsuits:

three were wholly successful; the fourth one was half successful—the only half that wasn't successful was the fact that state law did not permit the judge to fix what the state had broken.

ANDERSON: Mmm.

KRUSE: Right.

ABRAMS: So by the time we get to November 16, 2018, a different picture emerged. It was around November 14, when my campaign manager and I were talking, and we just knew that the pathway was narrower and narrower. This was in part because we knew that ballots had been thrown away, that provisional ballots had been discounted, that all of these other pieces had broken in the process. We decided we should talk about provisional ballots and what those meant to the outcome (more had been discovered, but the lack of record keeping meant we likely could not prove the total number discarded); but, by that time, I was thinking through what do I need to do? I was talking to one of my dearest friends, and he said, "Are you going to concede?" and I said . . . I was like, "I can't even say the word."

[Laughter]

ABRAMS: And so I was not running.

DOWNS: Right, right, okay.

[Laughter]

ABRAMS: But we were having this conversation—and he's one of my closest advisers—and he said, "Well, what do you mean?" And I said, "You know what concession means, and I can't spend ten days telling people that they need to fight for the right to have their voices heard and then say, 'Oops, never mind.'"

ANDERSON: Right.

ABRAMS: There's a legitimate concern that as a candidate I had talked to people and engaged them and said, "I'm a standard-bearer for your rights," and, therefore, my obligation wasn't to do what would be politically expedient for me. The question was what was the most effective way to make certain the result of the election didn't lead to despondency and disengagement.

ANDERSON: Yes.

ABRAMS: But instead led to righteous indignation and action.

KRUSE AND ANDERSON: Mmhmm.

ABRAMS: As we continued to talk, he said, "Well, what are you going to say?" And I said, "I acknowledge that he is going to have more votes by the end of the day because that's how he orchestrated the system."

ANDERSON: Mmhmm.

DOWNS: Right.

ABRAMS: And he said, "Well, is that what you're going to do?" And I said, "Well, I don't know, let me write it down."

ANDERSON: [Laughs]

ABRAMS: That night I wrote the speech, which was "Yes I acknowledge . . . As a matter of law I acknowledge." But then I wanted to talk about why concession was so dangerous; that my responsibility wasn't to make myself governor through this process; my responsibility was to make sure that the voters of Georgia were heard through this process, and that did not happen. And the word "concession" has meaning—it means it's true, and right, and proper.

ANDERSON: Yes.

ABRAMS: You could preserve the legitimacy of a democracy by acknowledging that the law allows this outcome without conceding the process itself. I anticipated what the rebuttal would be, which is that I would be called a sore loser, that I would . . . you know, "You'll never work in this town again."

[Laughter]

ABRAMS: And so the second part of the speech . . .

ANDERSON: "Angry black woman"?

ABRAMS: I mean, I'm an aloof, angry black woman. Yeah, they're really confused by how my anger works.

[Laughter]

ABRAMS: But the second part of my obligation was then to anticipate that response, which is that you're supposed to be stoic. But stoicism essentially allows them to continue. That grace that you're supposed to demonstrate is really, sort of, you're stiffening your back as they beat you.

ANDERSON: Yeah.

ABRAMS: And then the silence is consent. It is allowing the legitimacy of the action, and my speech was not going to do that, because the goal was to say to the voters, "I'm never going to become governor under this current regime, but that doesn't delegitimize the work you did to show up to try to make it so."

DOWNS: Great, so one of the other questions I have that goes back to something that Heather mentioned—Heather Cox Richardson—about the Motor Voter Law, is—and this is not to make this conversation into a reflection on Carol's book . . .

[Laughter]

DOWNS: So I don't know if this came from your book or if I saw this when you were on *The Daily Show*, but it was some image that you paint. It's in Alabama.

ANDERSON: Oh.

DOWNS: You mention a recording of Republicans behind closed doors saying, "We don't want the HUD buses to be pulling up and bringing people to the polls." And so I'm just thinking about how buses of people from HUD evokes a particular image in the American imagination . . .

ANDERSON: Yes.

DOWNS: And when people see HUD buses arriving to the polls on the news, it then makes voting among poor black people appear as a privilege, not as a right.

ANDERSON: John Merrill, who is the secretary of state in Alabama, has called it a privilege, as has Kris Kobach, the secretary of state out of Kansas, so you're looking at a couple of the kings of voter suppression who look at a right as a privilege. And so the recording dealt with, there was a law dealing with something like gambling or something, and so they were trying to figure out how to maneuver this thing through and shut it down, and they said, "How do we depress the black voter turnout? Because all of these aborigines and these illiterates will get on these HUD-financed busses and go to the polls." And I think that's important to understand because one of the things that we're dealing with when we're dealing with voter suppression is a stereotypical narrative about who black people are.

KRUSE AND DOWNS: Right.

ANDERSON: So that's why when they talk about "stealing the election," they point to cities. They point to St. Louis. Trump pointed to Philadelphia. This is where they're pointing. Because in cities in our national imagination, cities are where black people are, and this is where crime is, and so when you have stealing elections, black people, crime, it just seems to work together psychologically.

DOWNS: Right.

ANDERSON: So again, this "HUD-financed busses," "oh, they're on welfare, they're getting a handout," and this gets to "well, why don't they have enough initiative to just go vote?" So you see these components in there. So what they did in Alabama is—they did many things in Alabama and we'll get to moral turpitude—

[Laughter]

ANDERSON: So what they did in Alabama was they crafted a voter ID law in 2011, but they knew that it was so racist that it could not get through the Department of Justice preclearance review. Then *Shelby County v. Holder* came through and gutted the Voting Rights Act and gutted preclearance and [snaps fingers], boom, they implemented that voter ID law. Now when they implemented it, the NAACP Legal Defense Fund looked at it because it said you need to have government-issued photo ID, and they looked, and they said, "Yes, but we see you don't have public-housing ID on this list, and does it get more government issued than public housing?"

DOWNS: Right.

ANDERSON: And Alabama's retort was "no, that's not an acceptable form of government-issued photo ID." But in Alabama—because Alabama is a very poor state, it's somewhere between forty-fifth and forty-eighth in the nation in terms of poverty—71 percent of those in public housing are African American, and as the Legal Defense Fund noted, for many, that's the only ID they have. They don't have cars; cars are expensive, and if you are poor, you can't afford a car.

DOWNS: Right.

ANDERSON: So when you cancel the one ID, the one government-issued photo ID that people have, then you are blocking their access to the ballot box, but you're doing so in a way where you don't have to be Sheriff Jim Clark. Then Governor [Robert] Bentley shut down the Department of Motor Vehicles in the black belt counties, which are the counties where you have sizable numbers of African Americans living. So if you can't use your government-issued photo ID from public housing, and you don't have a driver's license bureau to get the driver's license to be able to vote, so you have to go like fifty miles to be able to get a driver's license, but if you don't drive—and Alabama is ranked forty-eighth in the nation in terms of public transportation—so if you don't drive, and you don't have public transportation, how do you then get the driver's license that you need in order to be able to vote? And so this is why it is such, what I call this kind of quiet slow burn, because you don't see it but these very quiet bureaucratic mechanisms that are really undergirded—and this is one of the pieces I think we need to pull out here—it's really undergirded by what happened to the Republican Party with the southern strategy.

DOWNS: That's my next question.

THOMPSON: But I also think it's really important to put the actors back into this process, because one of the problems of talking about it in terms of Supreme Court decisions or local ordinances is it seems even less real—it seems even less vibrant—and, you know, the violence that's committed by doing those acts is violence. When you refused to concede, that was calling it for what it was, and I think we still—again the public but I think even historians—we have a hard time . . . if someone is not saying, "We're not going to take this ID because we hate black people," even as historians . . .

KRUSE: Yeah.

DOWNS: Yeah.

THOMPSON: We have a hard time being able to connect those dots without a lot of inference, and that's where this is so critical that we point out that those kind of acts, they're not benign.

They're not banal. They're not just "happening," passive-voice happening—there's actors that are making them happen.

ANDERSON: Yes, yes.

THOMPSON: And that in fact, if we had everyone voting in Alabama, that the most fundamental power relations would be completely upended.

ANDERSON: Ooo.

RICHARDSON: In terms of class . . .

ANDERSON: Ooo.

THOMPSON: And race . . .

ANDERSON: Hoo!

THOMPSON: And gender, it would look exactly like it did in the fifties or the sixties because you would see dead people, and you would see arms, because that's what's at stake, and I think not . . . for us to not keep calling out what's at stake here is one of the biggest silences of all.

RICHARDSON: Can I build on that though? There's something even larger at stake, and that's American democracy.

ANDERSON: Yes.

RICHARDSON: Because we're all talking as if people should vote, but obviously the people that don't want certain other people to vote are not behind the project of democracy. One of the things you said earlier is about assumptions people make and that assumptions are within the system. People who have created legislation have done it in such a way that it automatically reads some people out, and we are not even aware of that. So for example, right now we're talking about African Americans, but the Fourteenth Amendment excluded Indians not taxed.

KRUSE: Mmhmm.

ANDERSON: Yes.

RICHARDSON: And that was quite deliberate. And then in the Fifteenth Amendment, Nevada said, "We won't have anything to do with the Fifteenth Amendment until we make sure that it doesn't cover Chinese and Indians."

ANDERSON: Exactly.

RICHARDSON: And then across the West, they were like, "Oh sure, we're totally cool with the Fourteenth and Fifteenth Amendment; that's no problem at all," because in 1798 through 1802 we wrote all these citizenship laws that said only free white people could be citizens, so then you've just written off all the Indians, all the Asians, and usually the Mexicans.

ANDERSON: Yes.

KRUSE: Mmhmm.

RICHARDSON: And that whole idea that people—you talked about being "good citizens" so you would go and do these things—the idea that only certain people are Americans.

ANDERSON: Yes.

RICHARDSON: And those ideas are based on color, gender, almost always class, and certain ways of behavior and are deeply, deeply encoded in American law and in American ideology.

ANDERSON: Yes.

RICHARDSON: And so when we talk about specific laws need to be challenged, well, great, let's challenge a few laws, but that's not the point. The point is we need . . . not even necessarily a new language because there is at least one occasion in which we had it before—we had it during the Civil War and we had it during World War II—we need to revive the idea that democracy really does need to stand against fascism and communism, and it's going to create a world in which everybody has the right to self-determination. And until people buy into that . . . well, let's tinker with laws but . . .

THOMPSON: Well, that's why . . . voter suppression, which often doesn't bring people along because it's fundamentally about race, but it's also, as you just pointed out, it's so much bigger than that. True, right? I mean, if you're transgender, you are likely not going to vote because of your ID problems; if you are married and took your spouse's last name . . .

ANDERSON: Mmm.

RICHARDSON: You're out!

KRUSE: Right.

THOMPSON: You are unlikely to be able to vote. I mean, in fact, it is suppressing all of . . . honestly the most marginalized citizens in society.

RICHARDSON: How about the majority!

THOMPSON: One second. So by talking about it as a democracy, it also forces us to talk about suppression even more broadly.

ANDERSON: One of the things that I laid out in the 2016 election epilogue in *White Rage* was that what Trump was marketing was a neo-apartheid state, where you could create a vast labor pool of rightless people—of African Americans by using the police force so that as you rise up for your rights, you're dealing with massive police violence; for the Latino population by the pressure of ICE and deportation so that as you rise up, you're then dealing with the power of the state—so once you create this rightless, cowed population of labor that is doing that work, those resources that they generate then flow up to a category of whites. But what happened in that election is folks thought they were in on the con, and they were actually the mark, because it is a very narrowed band of whites that were to benefit from this system. But that was the vision, that was the drive, that was the pool. When Steve King out of Iowa—congressman out of Iowa—says, "You know, there were times when you used to have to own property to be able to vote," you're beginning to see the conception of what citizenship looks like. Particularly when you think about what happened after the Great Recession and what happened to black ownership of property, where fewer than 50 percent of African Americans owned a home. So when you start talking about owning property to be a citizen in order to be able to vote, you don't have to say race . . .

RICHARDSON: Yes, that's exactly right.

ANDERSON: Because it's said. And so these are the kind of layers—it's "not the public-housing ID, but you have to have a driver's license," or in North Dakota it's "your ID has to have an address on it," knowing good and doggone well that those who live on reservations do not have street addresses. So you write the code in a way to define citizens, and that's what's happening. So that's why what happened in Florida with that incredible ballot initiative, issue 4, was so tremendous.

KRUSE: Yeah.

ANDERSON: Because, as Heather said, you had 6.2 million Americans who had lost their right to vote because they had been disfranchised because of a felony conviction.

DOWNS: Right.

ANDERSON: 1.7 million of them were in Florida alone.

THOMPSON: That's right.

ANDERSON: So when 1.7 million . . . And so this allows Florida to basically have what I call like the three-fifths compromise, where they're counting the folks in order to get the representatives in Congress.

THOMPSON: And we're not even talking about prison gerrymandering, which is a whole separate issue.

[Chattering]

ANDERSON: Exactly.

THOMPSON: In all of the . . . in all but four states.

ANDERSON: Right, right, and so, what this did, though, is that you have the people saying . . . you know when Rick Scott as governor then really rigged the system to slow down reenfranchisement to a dribble.

KRUSE: Right.

ANDERSON: Then you have the people going, "Okay, we have tried it your way—it's not working. We are going to have some real democracy up in this house." And they began to organize and got that initiative through and got, what, 64 percent?

KRUSE: Amazing.

THOMPSON: Wow.

KRUSE: Yeah, I couldn't believe the numbers when they rolled in.

ANDERSON: Right, 64 percent of the vote in order to reenfranchise 1.4 million Floridians.

DOWNS: Right.

ANDERSON: Think about what a game changer that is, particularly in a swing state like Florida. But this is . . . it's to say, "A dying mule kicks hardest," so you're now looking at the legislature now coming back and saying, "But you've got to pay all of your court fees and fines."

KRUSE: Right.

RICHARDSON: Mmm.

THOMPSON: Right.

ANDERSON: So you've got, basically.

KRUSE AND ANDERSON: A poll tax!

DOWNS: Yeah.

THOMPSON: That's right.

RICHARDSON: Can you explain a bit more about prison gerrymandering and the felony stuff?

THOMPSON: So we talk all the time about felony disfranchisement, and that tends to be where especially the media spends most of its attention, if it's going to spend any at all, on the issue of voter suppression these days. But in countless counties, states, areas, there are . . . there's an in some respects to me a much more insidious kind of voter suppression going on that is much more like the three-fifths clause: prison gerrymandering. So take my city of Detroit: when folks are arrested in the overwhelmingly black city of Detroit, they are then shipped to an upstate Michigan prison, in an overwhelmingly white upstate county, where their body counts for census population in that upstate county. This has huge implications. It's a double whammy. Not only can these people not vote while locked in that upstate prison (like they can in other countries such as Albania, Denmark, Serbia, or Spain), but their bodies adding to the census count of that upstate county actually gives the white residents of that county a disproportionate political advantage. It gives them more political power than they actually merit given the one-person, one-vote rule. Also, there are other key resources that are attached to census population, right? Higher census numbers equals more federal and state monies for things like child nutrition programs. That matters a lot. When Detroit fell below a million people—when any area falls below a million people—that's devastating financially in the census. So everyone talks about white flight out of Detroit—well, that's a very real thing, but they're not talking about the fact that mass incarceration also emptied out this city . . . I think out of nine or eight of the counties that most people return to from prison, it's in Wayne County, which is Detroit.

ANDERSON: Mmhmm.

THOMPSON: So this form of voter suppression, as hidden as it is, all adds up, essentially, to a very real sucking of power and resources out of our nation's most marginalized areas to its already privileged areas. It's literally the case that every black body in a northern Michigan prison directly empowers white guards. They have more political power to get their candidate in office.

RICHARDSON: When did that start?

THOMPSON: Well, we've always counted prisoners as census population where they are locked up, not where they live . . . This is not new. But when it really began to distort our democracy, it's only become such a problem, in lieu of mass incarceration.

RICHARDSON: Right.

ANDERSON: Mmhmm.

THOMPSON: And again, this has a dramatic impact . . . I mean, in Pennsylvania key House and Senate districts would not exist if it weren't for prison gerrymandering. They wouldn't exist! It would violate the one-person, one-vote law. Same thing with other states. I think Michigan it's, like, four of them. Georgia, what's Georgia's?

ABRAMS: So, we have . . . and it gets even worse because we have private prisons.

KRUSE: Mmhmm.

ABRAMS: So there are a handful of counties in South Georgia where there would be a sparse population but for the prisoners and the guards.

ANDERSON: Mmhmm.

ABRAMS: In certain parts of Georgia, counties have a *small* population, particularly in South Georgia. In these rural counties, where you see substantive depopulation, they will not access resources but for a rigged census count. I just launched an organization called Fair Count because we won't be able to address the challenges there until we undo the structure of the legislature. But the only counterweight is to increase the counts in those communities, so going into a place like Detroit or Atlanta and making certain that the census count is accurate because the hardest-to-count populations are immigrants, people of color, the poor, renters, and children, all the communities that require the highest amount of resources for their sufficiency to be made real and manifest, and thus they are the very same folks who are the victims of disenfranchisement.

KRUSE: Mmhmm.

RICHARDSON: Right.

ABRAMS: Because it's all of the piece.

THOMPSON: Right, but, for example, in Michigan, you don't lose your right to vote when you come home, so people think, "Oh, Michigan is in a much better position," but it actually isn't, because of its prison gerrymandering. So that's an example of . . . it's a second layer of the whole voter suppression thing that no one talks about, and it's complicated, I mean, because it really is state based. New York had prison gerrymandering too; it had a dramatic impact in Upstate New York, and Republican state legislators would say very publicly, "You know it's a good thing prisoners can't vote 'cause if they could they wouldn't vote for me."

[Scoffing, chuckling]

THOMPSON: You know, they were absolutely clear about it. But the good news is that people worked to get rid of prison gerrymandering in New York; they got rid of it in Maryland. So it's possible to undo, but even then . . .

ABRAMS: You have to change the voting rights.

THOMPSON: Right, exactly.

KRUSE: Right, right.

DOWNS: So what happened in Florida with the prison case this past year?

ABRAMS: It's still pending.

THOMPSON: Yeah, it's not resolved, right?

ABRAMS: So the legislature is in session right now. The bill they've put forward is making its way through the House, and it would impose . . . that you'd have to pay all fees and fines before restoration was real.

RICHARDSON: Mmhmm.

ABRAMS: And it advanced out of committee, I think, this week, so it's on the path to passage. [*The bill passed and was signed into law by the governor of Florida after this conversation took place.*]

THOMPSON: And let's be clear that even if someone does have the right to vote, even if you've restored voting rights upon release, people don't believe they have the right to vote.

ABRAMS: Yes.

RICHARDSON: Right.

THOMPSON: And also, of course, the studies are very clear that once you have this many negative interactions with the state, the absolute last place you want to go is to give your information to an officer of the state.

KRUSE: Right.

ANDERSON: Yeah. This is where, though, I think . . . in the book that last chapter is on what I call the resistance.

DOWNS: Right.

ANDERSON: And I deal with Alabama and the Doug Jones / Roy Moore special Senate race. And so, for instance in 1901 Alabama's Constitution, Jim Crow Constitution, had a clause in there that if you have been convicted of a crime of moral turpitude, then you will not be able to vote.

DOWNS: Right.

ANDERSON: But Alabama refused to define "moral turpitude." But if you had been convicted of a crime of moral turpitude and you tried to vote, you could be hit with a felony and go to prison, and so, you're caught in this really crazy catch-22, because you don't know whether your crime is actually moral turpitude.

RICHARDSON AND KRUSE: Mmhmm.

ANDERSON: And it took incredible efforts from civil society, League of Women Voters, NAACP Legal Defense Fund, ACLU, pounding on Alabama for decades. In 2017, Alabama finally defined moral turpitude.

RICHARDSON: What was it?

ANDERSON: Rape, murder, treason, I mean, the biggies, right?

RICHARDSON AND KRUSE: Mmhmm.

ANDERSON: Drug crimes, *not* moral turpitude. And so then the organizations turned to John Merrill, secretary of state, and said, "Great, all of those people that you told could not vote"—because by that time it was something like 8 percent of Alabama's adult population could not vote because of moral turpitude, and 15 percent of its black adult population—and Merrill said, "Eh, no, I'm not going to do that [let people know they can vote]. I don't think it's a good use of state resources." Now think about that when you have the secretary of state, who had no problem telling people that they could not vote because of moral turpitude, now because of the new law saying, "That's not a good use of state resources."

DOWNS: Right.

KRUSE: Mmhmm.

RICHARDSON: Never mind.

ANDERSON: And so here civil society, again, stepped up.

DOWNS: Right.

ANDERSON: The ACLU and the Legal Society of Alabama, they stepped in and set up restoration clinics. And what the story is about is that there is a way to defeat these folks.

DOWNS: Right.

ANDERSON: First thing they did was, via social media and on radio, they issued notices; "Hey, there's a new law. You might actually have your voting rights."

DOWNS: Right.

ANDERSON: "Come, come, let us look. We'll find out, and we'll get you your voting rights back." So, the first place they set it up was in Selma.

DOWNS: Right.

ANDERSON: That was the first restoration clinic. And you had a team of lawyers going through the conviction records going, "Nope, not moral turpitude, not moral turpitude, not moral turpitude." Then you had a team of volunteers going through all of Alabama's voter registration laws to get folks registered to vote. And then they had caravans, because they knew there were some folks who were not going to step foot in a church, and so they have these caravans going to these poor communities with all of this information, again doing the same thing. And Alabama had a law where if you were in jail, you could actually vote absentee as long as you hadn't been convicted of a crime of moral turpitude.

DOWNS: That's right.

ANDERSON: But if you're sitting in jail, you're like [chuckling], "I'm not voting..."

THOMPSON: I think it's extraordinary historically, and I'm thinking right now of Pippa Holloway's book on disfranchisement (*Living in Infamy: Felon Disfranchisement and the History of American Citizenship*), it's the extraordinary efforts ordinary human beings have gone to to get their rights to vote back.

ANDERSON: Yes.

THOMPSON: And the desire people have to exercise their right to vote, which actually leads me to ask a question of you, Stacey... What is the fallout of having an election such as your recent election, where people work so hard and you are so right to call it out? What happened? What's the followup so that it's not, "So then screw it"?

ABRAMS: One of the things is the way we talk about suppression. When suppression is seen as inevitable, then it's a reason not to try.

KRUSE: Right.

ABRAMS: And so part of it is the language that we use. We talk about it as an activity that you have to fight voter suppression—you have to fight back against it—because these are the populations that are the most likely to give up because of obstacles. Two is that we spend a lot of time connecting the right to vote to actual policies. The abstract notion of voting to those that live in intergenerational poverty, who've been incarcerated, it is so remote as to have no meaning, and so we spend a great deal of work through our organization Fair Fight Action actually connecting the right to vote to a real issue that they face.

KRUSE: Mmhmm.

ABRAMS: If you live in a community . . . the state of Georgia refused to expand Medicaid. If you live in a rural community without a hospital, and now you're more likely to die of a stroke because it takes two hours to get to the help you need, the fact that a person was elected that does not believe you have access to healthcare, that's a direct result of the right to vote.

ANDERSON: Right.

RICHARDSON: Mmhmm.

DOWNS: Wow.

ABRAMS: But we are obligated to connect the dots.

KRUSE: Right.

THOMPSON: That's one of the challenges.

ABRAMS: One of the challenges . . . the New Georgia Project, which was our voter registration effort that started in 2014, actually came about because of the Affordable Care Act. In 2013, Georgia was one of the states that refused the federal funding for the navigators to help people sign up for the ACA for the first time. If you lived in Atlanta, the metro Atlanta area, that wasn't a problem because philanthropists and existing nonprofits, they would fill in the gaps, and there would be enough people to go through those communities. South Georgia is largely rural, poor, and deeply in need of healthcare, but you also have huge swaths of the population that never had health insurance.

KRUSE: Right.

ABRAMS: They did not understand the process. I'd had this nonprofit I started in law school; and I sort of rejiggered it, called it the New Georgia Project, raised some money, and hired sixty people from within those communities, got a group to come down and train them, and they became the navigators or the prenavigators to get people signed up.

RICHARDSON: Mmhmm.

ABRAMS: But in the process, they would knock on doors and get folks in households signed up. But you would have someone in the household who could sign up for ACA, but there were folks who were too poor for the ACA, and Georgia refused Medicaid expansion. And they said President Obama did not give them healthcare. They did not understand that it was the governor and the state legislators that represented them who rejected Medicaid. In a lot of these communities, the person denying them access was also their high school football coach, who was also the state legislator. And so what I realized was "okay, so they don't understand how government works."

RICHARDSON: Right.

THOMPSON: Right.

ABRAMS: I mean there are people in government who don't know how government works. And so the shift became that instead of simply doing the work of navigation, I wanted to get these people involved in the body politic; only they weren't registered.

RICHARDSON: Yeah.

ABRAMS: We know that third-party voter registration is essential for getting low-income and communities of color to register to vote because they will not register unless they are asked because the process seems too complicated and fraught with peril.

[Murmurs of approval]

ABRAMS: These are not communities that are going to intentionally go or have the resources to go and seek out information. And so we went to them, and we registered them to vote. In Georgia in 2014, there were eight hundred thousand nonregistered people of color, six hundred thousand of whom were African American. These were people who were eligible to vote but who had never been registered or had been registered but were kicked off the rolls. And so the way we talk about voter suppression, the way we talk about engagement, the way all of the work is grounded is that you have to meet people where they are, not where you want them to be.

ANDERSON: Yes.

ABRAMS: But you also have to give them real-life examples of why change is possible, and that's the last thing I'll add. Third-party registration is one of the other pieces of voter suppression that we don't talk about enough. The average . . . the wealthy person who gets registered to vote will vote more than 50 percent of the time. The middle-class person who registers to vote will vote roughly 30–50 percent of the time. A poor person who registers to vote will vote 20 percent of the time or less, in part because it's like handing someone the keys to a car . . . or, sorry, handing someone a driver's license but never teaching them how to drive or giving them a car. And so the act of being registered is a huge dramatic step because this population is also the least likely to vote unless a third party asks. That's why Texas and Florida took the steps . . .

ANDERSON: Yes.

ABRAMS: In Texas it is essentially illegal for third parties to register voters.

ANDERSON: Yeah.

ABRAMS: That means all of those communities we hear about who need to be registered to vote.

ANDERSON: Yes, yes, yes.

ABRAMS: It is deeply hard to get it done. In Florida they did the same, you had to . . . you had seventy-two hours to return the form; if you didn't, you'd go to jail. The League of Women Voters pulled out of doing voter registration in Florida for a time.

KRUSE AND ANDERSON: Mmhmm.

ABRAMS: And so across the country you see more and more laws that are being put in place to eliminate third-party registration.

And the reason ... so to your point, the reaction has been people are angry, but they aren't despondent. And the opportunity is to make certain that we channel that anger into action but never talk about it as an inevitability, because when voter suppression is seen as inevitable, people believe it and they stay home.

DOWNS: Can I just pick up on that point, channeling the anger into action? And I'm thinking about my own favorite story of voting or the most memorable one in my mind was the 2004 election. Because Bush was about to be reelected and I was really hoping that he would not be reelected, I went to the polls early in the morning. I was in graduate school, and I voted for John Kerry, the Democrat nominee, and he lost. The next day I was in the library at my carrel working with my friends on our dissertations, and I was so despondent, I remembering saying, "What happened?" And people just said to me, "Oh, we all need time to process. We need time to think about it." And I'm wondering now how the uptick in protest, particularly the activism sparked by Black Lives Matter, has invigorated people. How has the current political moment changed the reaction to voter suppression from "let's process" to "let's do something"? Has the rise in activism actually helped to illuminate the problems of voter suppression? Because, for me, in 2004, I was very frustrated with the outcome of election, but there was nowhere for me to go. There was nothing to do. There were few networks to tap into ... I don't know if it's a silver lining to this terrible problem, but has the resurgence of political activism inspired people to respond to the problems of voter suppression?

KRUSE: I think if there is a silver lining to our current moment, it's that people have stopped taking democracy for granted.

ANDERSON: Yes.

KRUSE: I think a lot of this country has been on autopilot for the last couple decades of a sense of "nothing really matters, it doesn't really affect me, I don't really benefit off of this, I don't have any skin in the game." And what we've seen, certainly in the last two years through the #MeToo movement, through Black Lives Matter, through the March for Our Lives after Parkland, you've seen a real reawakening of what it means to be a citizen, and that it's not simply showing up to the polls every four years, as most people thought, and, "Well, I'll be back to vote again in four," or maybe you were good enough to come every two years, maybe you were good enough to vote in local elections. Now there's a real sense that it's not just about showing up on election day but actually being engaged *every* day—writing your congressman, talking to your mayor, showing up to meetings, town halls, being a presence, stepping up, and that there's an active role for people to be involved in.

ANDERSON: Yes.

KRUSE: And this is why I think your point [Kruse gestures to Abrams] about politicians conceding is really vital because all too often that moment says, "Well, we're done. You came out and fought, and it didn't matter. I'm not going to fight for you," and instead to really lean into that and say, "There are a lot of issues here that are ongoing and need to be addressed," and I think what we've seen and you saw it in the midterms in 2018.

ANDERSON: Hooo.

KRUSE: Voter turnout was amazing!

ANDERSON: Yes!

KRUSE: But it's got to be sustained.

ANDERSON: Yes.

KRUSE: It can't be a one-off. It can't be something that happens every two years. You've got to see . . . again we saw just recently, that state supreme court election in Wisconsin. Democrats assumed that Wisconsin's back in the blue column and there's nothing to do. It was an incredibly close race. I don't know if they've called it yet, but it was much closer than it should have been. So it requires not just stepping up to vote but being vigilant and really realizing that there's a lot that everyone has to gain and also a lot to lose.

THOMPSON: And also historians, I have to say, this not to pat ourselves on the back as historians at the table, but there has been a real shift there too, which is that historians are much more in the public on the news channels talking, writing for major outlets, and sometimes it feels like we're all talking to each other, but I think it does shift the public discourse. At least someone is responding when someone says there's this crisis at the border or voter fraud. There actually is a response not just on party lines, not just at the political level.

DOWNS: Well, I was going to ask—

RICHARDSON: Well, can I just . . .

DOWNS: Go ahead.

RICHARDSON: Can I just go back to the concept of democracy again? One of the things that has astonished me and got me into this profession and has kept me in this profession is that from the time of Goldwater on but really from Reagan on is that the GOP has not hidden that it is trying to destroy the liberal consensus, which is actually really popular.

ANDERSON: Yes.

RICHARDSON: They have said so. They have said, "We are going to get rid of Medicare and Medicaid. We are going to get rid of the Great Society. We are going to get rid of everything right back to the 1920s."

ANDERSON: Yes.

RICHARDSON: There's a very clear line of this, and no matter how much you shouted that people are like, "Nah, they don't mean it. They don't really mean it."

[Laughter]

RICHARDSON: "They're not going to attack . . ."—I heard that last week—"they're not *really* going to go after Medicare."

KRUSE: Mmhmm.

ANDERSON: Ahh . . .

RICHARDSON: And I think what happened is, what I see now feels very much to me—and I say feels interestingly enough because I live in the nineteenth century—feels very much to me like the 1850s.

ANDERSON: Yeah.

RICHARDSON: Where people could say, "Oh no, the slave owners really aren't going to do *that!* They aren't going to do *that!*" Finally, the penny dropped in 1854 when the Democrats, the southern Democrats who ran the Democratic Party, said, "Well, yeah, we really are going to take over the country."

[Chuckling]

RICHARDSON: "We really are going to spread slavery across the West, and we're going to overrule the North, and we're going to start this great slaveholding center of power for the world, and this is good!" The Cornerstone Speech says this is the next phase of American society, or even of human society, and democracy was wrong. James Henry Hammond, who was a southerner, a South Carolina senator, gives his famous speech in 1858 about how most people are dumb "mudsills" who need guidance from their betters, and then the Cornerstone Speech, of course—Alexander Stephens's speech about the basis of the Confederacy—they both say, "This is the wave of the future.

The Founders had it wrong when they said all men are created equal." Of course, the Founders were only talking about men—they hadn't included women yet, but women could fit into that concept—and the southern leaders really believe that it's their job to tear that equality down. It's in 1854 when it becomes clear that Americans who totally disagree about immigration, totally disagree about internal improvements, totally disagree about whether their party or the other party should be in power say: "Stop. We disagree about all of this stuff, but if we don't stop this rising oligarchy and reestablish democracy..."

ANDERSON: Mmhmm.

RICHARDSON: We are all sixteen thousand different kinds of... I'm not going to use the word I'm thinking of here. So I was fascinated by Black Lives Matter because, you know, police officers have been killing black people forever. It made the news in a huge way back in the early 1980s with Jeffrey Dahmer, who was a serial killer who, um... I'm not going to go into great detail there because people are going to read this.

DOWNS: Oh, God, not Jeffrey Dahmer...

THOMPSON: Yeah.

RICHARDSON: : And you know, black people had called the police again and again and again on Dahmer, and the cops looked the other way. Once they even returned one of his victims. So black people looked at how little the police cared about their lives and said you know, "Reagan took all our jobs. Congress took our programs, and now white people are literally *eating us*, and you're still not doing anything." And even today, if you look up Jeffrey Dahmer, people don't realize that he largely preyed on...

ANDERSON: People of color.

RICHARDSON: People of color, especially black people. So the lack of concern about black lives has been visible forever—and certainly since the very public Dahmer case—but Black Lives Matter, it seemed to me, was the moment where the system's treatment of black men caught the national attention because a lot of people who didn't care about police brutality, didn't care about young black men, didn't care about people they perceived as criminals said, "Oh, wait a minute. Next it's going to be me." And we are now at a moment where people are saying, "I care deeply about what's happening to immigrant children at the border because we know how this goes. We saw this happen in 1939."

ANDERSON: Yes.

RICHARDSON: "And it's only a question of time before it's me." So I see this as one of those moments when American democracy is absolutely on a razor's edge, and people are coming out to call it back.

ABRAMS: And I think that's why it's important that we talk about voter suppression as an act of corrosion, as a corrosive act to democracy. The other challenge I get is that I tend to say, "Look, our democracy is resilient, but it's vulnerable."

ANDERSON: Mmhmm.

ABRAMS: And that voter suppression is a crisis of democracy. And people are like, "Well, no, democracy's not in crisis." Yes.

RICHARDSON: Yeah.

ABRAMS: If people cannot be heard in a democracy, it's no longer a democracy. But I think one of the spaces where historians are so vital is that it's not only the reminder of what we've done, it's a reminder of the meaning of what we've done. And so one opportunity I think heading into 2020 is for historians to be part of the debate stage, actually crafting questions and framing things in terms of real . . . I would even go so far as to say you should ask to host a debate.

DOWNS: That's right.

[Chuckling]

DOWNS: I'm serious! We should host a debate.

ABRAMS: Because a debate that's hosted by historians who actually know what they're talking about and didn't read it on Wikipedia before going onstage . . .

DOWNS: Right.

[Laughter]

ABRAMS: Would be transformative, because you could provide context.

THOMPSON: [Jokingly] They would decline to come!

RICHARDSON: I was going to say, "Can you imagine?"

THOMPSON: "No thanks!"

ABRAMS: You've never been a politician who wants to be on the stage.

[Chuckling]

DOWNS: Right, right.

ABRAMS: But my larger point is the role that history can play, the fact that when you said the Cornerstone Speech, I thought, "I remember that, but the last time I thought about it was when I had a teacher telling me it was a really good idea because I grew up in Mississippi."

[Sighing and grumbling]

ABRAMS: I mean he didn't say it out loud, but he was really sad. But there is a space for the education of those who seek to be entrusted with democracy to be reminded of the harm that can be done if we do not understand.

THOMPSON: Or the power of activism because, going to Stacey's point about activism, you know even in high schools or junior highs when we're teaching the civil rights era and the voting rights era, it's very much a top-down narrative, right? One day Lyndon Johnson wakes up and he's like, "Damn that's a good idea. Let's pass some civil rights laws."

ABRAMS: Well, he talked to MLK before he did it.

THOMPSON: That's true, but . . .

ABRAMS: Yeah, just the two of them.

THOMPSON: But we should be reminded that like Black Lives Matter today, people didn't have any choice but to weigh in on these debates and change them, so that's also empowering, to connect that point about how people feel in power. They . . . Oftentimes today I think students don't feel empowered because they have this imagination about what it was before.

ANDERSON: Yes.

THOMPSON: And yeah, the small pressures cumulatively make people with power move . . . I mean, I was at a convening of prosecutors, and this was in the wake of Ferguson, and for the first time one of the big discussions at the table was "how many police shootings are in our districts? And why?" Not because, well, many of them maybe cared, but they were also terrified! They didn't want Boston to blow up. They didn't want Baltimore to blow up, you know? And so I think you have to connect those dots of the activism piece to history, that's empowering.

ANDERSON: Right, and one of the things I know I do in my classes, because sometimes this really looks dark and daunting, is I also talk about the folks who stood up with the courage of their convictions because that is also so key. So it's Hugh Thompson who puts his helicopter between Lieutenant Calley's troops and the

South Vietnamese at My Lai; it is Edward Morel who takes on the King of Belgium to stop what is happening in the Congo.

KRUSE: Yeah.

ANDERSON: I mean, that kind of courage is absolutely essential, and when I'm teaching the movement, I'm teaching it from the grassroots up.

THOMPSON: Which is what we do in college.

RICHARDSON: They're regular people.

ANDERSON: Yeah, these are regular folk who are just like, "Uh-uh." So, it is Vera Pigee in Clarksdale, Mississippi, whose beauty shop—because she had the independent economic power, because she was a hairdresser and she wasn't reliant on white customers and white banks in order to thrive—was able to have her space be where African Americans could go to organize around the right to vote, around the right to quality education. And so, understanding that, that's one of the things historians do.

DOWNS: Right.

KRUSE: And not just the individual side. The last lecture I give in my class is to remind these students who get caught up in that "great man" theory, and it usually is great *men*, because it's arguments like "LBJ and MLK made the civil rights movement, period."

THOMPSON: They did everything.

KRUSE: And when I teach it, I try to stress the story at the grassroots, but I come back in that last lecture to remind them that even those people that they think of as the "great men" started young, you know? Bob Moses was leading the Mississippi Freedom Summer when he was twenty-six. MLK launched the Montgomery bus boycott when he was twenty-five.

ANDERSON: Right, right.

KRUSE: That's how I tell the story of the sixties, you know? . . . Tom Haden founded Students for a Democratic Society when he was a college junior.

ANDERSON: Right.

KRUSE: Or Gordon Hirabayashi resisted the World War II curfew for Japanese Americans when he was a college senior. The Little Rock Nine we talked about, those were high school seniors, you know? Lillian Gobitas went to the Supreme Court to fight for religious freedom when she was in elementary school. So people often sit around waiting for the great man to show up without realizing *you* are the great man. *You* are the great woman. So step up for this moment.

ANDERSON: Yeah.

KRUSE: Step up because you can't wait for the big savior to come get you. It is individuals who do this.

ANDERSON: You are your savior. You are your savior. And I think then, "Why voter suppression?" Because voter suppression is absolutely corrosive to democracy. What we haven't talked about is extreme partisan gerrymandering, for instance.

KRUSE: Yeah.

ANDERSON: And what that has done. But what . . . when we lean into it, as you say, is that we understand that we get this incredible, an incredible sense . . . We rely on the aspirations of hope. That's where African Americans have consistently fought for their freedom. It has not been on what America is but what America could be.

[Murmurs of approval]

ANDERSON: And it is that vision of what could be, has been the thing that has created enormous power and drive into transforming this nation. And I think . . . and I will say—I don't think, I know—that this is why this is so frightening to the Republicans.

RICHARDSON: Of course.

ANDERSON: Because what the southern strategy did is they wooed that toxin of white supremacy into the party after '64—I mean really wooed it; I mean they'd been playing with it for '48 and '52 but really wooed it—was that they thought that they could handle it. It's like a drug; they thought that they could handle it, but it became more and more toxic, and it drove the moderate Republicans out. As it drove the moderates out, it moved the party's policies further and further to the right, where . . . it could no longer resonate with the diversity of America. So how do you win?

DOWNS: Right.

RICHARDSON: You change the voter base.

ANDERSON: You change the voter base. So, in our discussion about the threat to democracy, by changing the voter base what you have to do then is you have to eliminate the voices of the majority of Americans.

DOWNS: Right.

KRUSE: Right.

ANDERSON: And basically create minoritarian rule. Which is so
. . .

RICHARDSON: Oligarchy.

ANDERSON: Right, and that is why truly we are on this razor's edge, but I don't see folks giving up.

THOMPSON: Well, they're not giving up. In part, I think that they [gesturing to Abrams] . . . I love this message, though, of not being defeated but being empowered, and I think that another way to do that is to remind people that nothing ever stays the same, right? I mean it's not . . . Something's always going to change, so it's just really a question of which direction, and someone was saying earlier about history repeating itself, it repeats itself for the good as well as the bad. And I think we're in this moment now that I . . . well, the optimism in me says the Black Lives Matter moment is like the Selma moment or something like that, but the other way of thinking about it is we were here before or after the Civil War, right? I mean, four million newly freed people, what's the response? Criminalize them. Take away their right to vote as a key strategy, forced labor, all of that. And then, what happens right after 1965? The exact same thing. The two moments of mass incarceration after 1865 and after 1965. And that's not coincidental, but simultaneously—right?—there was a response to both of them, and weighing in on those moments to show that they don't stay forever.

ABRAMS: One of the things we, you know, the other flag in front of the bull that I do is I talk about the fact that we won the election.

ANDERSON: Mmhmm.

ABRAMS: The way I frame winning is it's the transformation of the electorate, despite the best intentions of the opposition.

KRUSE, ANDERSON, AND OTHERS: Mmhmm!

ABRAMS: We tripled Latino turnout because we actually engaged Latino voters, went to see them. We were the first campaign to do a bilingual canvas in Georgia.

RICHARDSON: Wow.

ABRAMS: To spend statewide on the gubernatorial race and do Spanish language ads. We actually built from the bottom up. We held convenings of not only activists from black, AAPI, or

Latino communities and marginalized groups but also journalists early on so that they were part of our campaign from the very beginning. Now they could cover us however they wanted, but they were part of the conversation. We also engaged activists early on because they had never been—in Georgia they weren't considered a part of either part of the electorate.

THOMPSON: Right.

ABRAMS: They weren't seen as a definitive vote. The same thing was true for the Asian American and Pacific Islander community, which is growing in Georgia—it's now about 4.5 percent of the population, but there was a . . . essentially a disinclination on the part of Democrats, and Republicans just assumed they were theirs.

KRUSE: Right.

ANDERSON: [Chuckling]

ABRAMS: So we were the first campaign to . . . you know, I went to the Korean community, I went to the Chinese community, and I'd been talking to these groups since my time in the legislature, but a big part of it was no one assumed it would help. I got 80 percent of the Asian and Pacific Islander vote in the state of Georgia. Nobody saw that coming, including me!

[Laughter]

THOMPSON: Right.

ABRAMS: And then there was the assumption that African Americans, that we'd maxed out, that if Obama hadn't gotten them, they weren't gettable.

ANDERSON: Mmhmm.

KRUSE: Right.

ABRAMS: We had 1.1 million Democrats voted in 2014; 1.2 million black people voted for me because we went to places where no one had shown up. And then the other argument, which is part of the southern strategy, was that by centering these communities of color, by centering these marginalized communities, you inherently alienate white voters.

ANDERSON: Mmm.

ABRAMS: I increased the white voter participation in Georgia for Democrats for the first time in a generation. And the reason I talk about that—and this goes to your point of optimism and hope—is the antidote to voter suppression is expanding the electorate. But that does not happen simply by saying, "They took your vote." There has to be an active obligation on the part of the candidates . . .

KRUSE: Right.

ABRAMS: And the apparatus to do that work, because otherwise oligarchy works.

RICHARDSON: Yeah.

ABRAMS: And it happens because we exempt ourselves—and I'm talking about we the politicians—we exempt ourselves from responsibility of actually building the electorate for the next candidate.

[Murmurs of approval]

ABRAMS: I can't build it just so I can win an election. I have to build an infrastructure that allows the next person, because I may not win.

RICHARDSON: Yeah.

ABRAMS: But if we have to rebuild it every time, there's a fight.

KRUSE: Right.

ANDERSON: Mmhmm.

THOMPSON: So important, yeah.

ABRAMS: And to your point about every four years, every two years, there's an election every day in Georgia.

[Laughter]

ABRAMS: We are electing to do something, and then we are voting on . . . I mean the water soil conservation district. "I don't know what that does"—I do, but—

ANDERSON: Yeah.

[Laughter]

ABRAMS: You know. But it's making certain that the antidote to suppression is not simply deconstruction of the laws to your point, but it's an animation of why it matters.

ANDERSON: Yes.

RICHARDSON: You did something else very important in 2018.

ABRAMS: Thank you.

RICHARDSON: And you weren't the only one. So obviously I look a lot at the ideas behind larger movements, and what was really interesting is most of the campaign videos from 2018 rejected the ideology of the movement conservatives since Reagan, which is the idea of the one guy out there taking care of his family and making it on his own. You and Amy McGrath and a whole bunch of other people offered a new vision of government. And it was fascinating because it was not a vision of government that was based on a single person, an individual. Your videos were the best in the sense that many people got up and talked about either their children or, a lot of them were veterans, so they talked about their units in Iraq and Afghanistan. Your videos were all about family without there being your own children involved. And it was very clearly an attempt—to me anyway, looking at it as a historian—an attempt to redefine the concept of government not as the cowboy conservatism of Barry Goldwater and Ronald Reagan but a new kind of community vision, and a community vision that was not based in a natal family, which was really important.

ANDERSON: Yes.

RICHARDSON: And that new articulation of a new system of government, and a government that looks very much, in a way, like the government of FDR, although he was doing something obviously quite different ...

KRUSE: Mmhmm.

RICHARDSON: Called for a government that addresses community needs.

ANDERSON: Yes.

RICHARDSON: It's an entirely new vision in American history and one that is extraordinarily exciting and works, I think, for the twenty-first century, when women are actually able to take a voice for the first time really since they started to split the gender gap in 1980.

THOMPSON: That's right.

ANDERSON: Absolutely, absolutely.

DOWNS: So we have about ten minutes left or so, and I can't believe that we've had this amazing and wonderful conversation, and we haven't even gotten to talk about *Shelby County v. Holder* in any kind of clear way.

[Laughter]

DOWNS: So I'm interested in any reflections on that because it's at the heart of voter suppression. It gutted the protections that the civil rights movement guaranteed, allowing states that had historic problems of disenfranchisement to no longer get federal preclearance to change their laws. It also, I think, dovetails with the idea that Heather Thompson brought up earlier: that sometimes historians are looking for certain kinds of evidence to prove that people in power have been targeting black people to disenfranchise them, but we often don't have that smoking gun. But in the case of voter suppression, we have historical evidence between the Mississippi Plan and *Holder*.

KRUSE: Yeah.

DOWNS: There's something like seven hundred other cases that Carol has counted of infractions. I remember first learning about this when I was watching *The Daily Show*, and you [gesturing to Anderson] said to Trevor Noah, "I realized I got a lot of work to do."

[Laughter]

DOWNS: And you heroically did all that work. I had no idea the DOJ had seven hundred cases before them to examine. So maybe if you, Carol, could just talk about that; then I'm going to open it up to the floor for two questions, and then we'll end.

ANDERSON: I'll just say that, to me, that what *Shelby County v. Holder* did, besides gutting section 4 of the Voting Rights Act, which dealt with defining who would come under preclearance, was that it hurled the United States back at least to 1957 and the Civil Rights Act of 1957. So now that all of the voting rights violations would have to be . . . would have to come through litigation . . .

DOWNS: Right.

ANDERSON: Which was a very long, costly, ineffective mode of dealing with voting rights violations, which was the reason why you had to have the 1965 Voting Rights Act.

KRUSE: Mmhmm.

ANDERSON: But it happened under the banner that had been this intellectual, conservative intellectual project that said racism is really no longer a force in America.

THOMPSON: Right.

DOWNS: That's right.

ANDERSON: That it's not that operating principle thing that it was in '65—"we have overcome."

THOMPSON: Right.

KRUSE: Mmhmm.

ANDERSON: And that required being blinded to evidence.

KRUSE: Right.

ANDERSON: So that the five justices didn't refuse to look at the re-authorization in 2006, where you had over seven hundred cases that the Department of Justice had blocked—changes that the Department of Justice had blocked—because they were racially discriminatory. So that can only happen if you're not paying attention to the evidence, which also leads us to where we are now where we're in a kind of alternative fact kind of world. But we refuse to be there. And so *Shelby County v. Holder* did enormous damage. I should also, I want to also say that remember in 2008 Obama's ground game brought 15 million new voters to the polls, overwhelmingly African American, Latino, Asian American, young, and poor. The GOP looked up, and one of them said, "Wow, what happened to all of the Republicans—did they all move to Utah?" Because those voters were going in the vast majority to Obama. Then in 2012 the black voter turnout exceeded the white voter turnout; 2013, we get *Shelby County v. Holder.*

[Murmurs of approval]

ANDERSON: This is not an accident. And that historical perspective allows us to see that when this voting population, when this democracy becomes as vibrant as it can be, as it should be, you have forces that are absolutely afraid of what that means for the kind of America that they're going to live in.

DOWNS: Right.

KRUSE: And there's a—

ABRAMS: And one thing I would mention—

THOMPSON: And one thing—

ABRAMS: Go ahead. [Gestures to Thompson]

THOMPSON: Just quickly. The very specific clamping down on black voting is really the key here because the actual percentage of ethnic voters, which I think is the way nonwhite voters are characterized, actually stayed the same in 2016. So what's noticeable is the drop in *black* voters specifically, just underscoring what you said. And this case is key to doing that—the crazy idea "race doesn't matter anymore," and also the school cases . . . beating back *Brown v. Board of Education*, beating back *Swann v. Mecklenburg*, beating back any of these. These legal assaults have ended up silencing it, black voters, black students, black communities, and I don't think people even realize that. Because more Latinos voted in 2016, the "ethnic" proportion of voters did not go down—it stayed the same—but what did drop dramatically was the black voters in that pool.

ANDERSON: Yeah, yeah.

ABRAMS: I think the other piece there is that it's the restoration of the county-unit system.

KRUSE: Yes.

ANDERSON: Mmm.

RICHARDSON: Yes, yes.

ABRAMS: And that's . . . for those who forget the history of the county-unit system, because counties are now allowed to operate essentially with their own versions of states' rights, . . . and that's why Senator McConnell reacted so strongly to the notion of federal oversight in HR 1 that would require there be uniformity in the administration of elections.

[Murmurs of approval]

ABRAMS: Because with the county-unit system back in place,

those rural counties that now get extra population would also have excess power and have no oversight, because part of what the Voting Rights Act required was preclearance from counties.

RICHARDSON: Exactly.

KRUSE: Mmhmm.

ANDERSON: That's right.

ABRAMS: And they can now operate with impunity because if your secretary of state believes what you're doing is right, you have no impediment and no obstacle to activating the level of voter suppression you need to see.

KRUSE: Right.

[Murmurs of approval]

ABRAMS: The example I will give is that Brian Kemp was secretary of state when the Quitman Ten . . . this group of largely black women, in a majority-black city, decided that they would help elect more black members to the school board. So they organized and used the absentee ballot system that Georgia has. When they were successful in electing a majority-black school board, the secretary of state and the governor, but the secretary of state initiated it, had the Georgia Bureau of Investigation go to these women's homes, and they were arrested. They all lost their jobs. The ones who had been rightfully elected were taken off of the school board by the governor. They went through multiple trials. One woman nearly committed suicide, and not a single person was convicted. But because the county was given the leeway to operate—and this actually preceded *Shelby v. Holder*—but the reality is it gives an imprimatur to counties to operate with impunity and with no recourse. The average person in one of those counties does not have the wherewithal to file suit.

KRUSE: This is what brings us back full circle. So what we have is . . . we all talk about *Shelby v. Holder*, but there's *another* Shelby County that starts this story off . . .

THOMPSON: Right.

ANDERSON: Yes.

KRUSE: The one in Tennessee, the Shelby County that gives us *Baker v. Carr*, where we get the idea of one person, one vote. [Gestures to Anderson] And I think we've really forgotten that this county imbalance was at the heart of our idea about equity and equality in voting rights. And *Baker v. Carr*, I think, is a story that I think historians haven't stressed enough. I mean, maybe in our classes we do, but I don't think the general public knows.

ANDERSON: No.

THOMPSON: No, I don't think so.

KRUSE: When Earl Warren was asked what the most important case in his tenure on the Supreme Court is, he didn't say *Brown v. Board*; he said *Baker v. Carr*.

ANDERSON: Mmhmm.

KRUSE: Because he knew how contentious and important that case was. I mean this was the case that basically broke the health of one justice and gave another one a stroke. Felix Frankfurter harassed Charles Whitaker into a nervous breakdown to the point where he had to leave the court, and then a month later Frankfurter himself is laid out with a stroke at his desk.

[Scattered laughter]

KRUSE: But it was that important of a decision, right?

ANDERSON: Yes, absolutely.

KRUSE: And it was one that got the court involved in politics. Before they'd said, "We don't have any role in politics," but here they finally said, "No, this is important. This is where democracy really is formed." And then you get in the Georgia case over the county unit—for folks who don't know the county-unit system was a Georgia system that gets put in place in 1917. Georgia's got 159 counties, and they set it up in 1917. They say, "You can either have six votes, four votes, or two votes," and they do it based on the population in 1917. They never update it!

ANDERSON: Right!

KRUSE: That imbalance stays in place, even as the cities undergo tremendous growth. So by the time you get to the early sixties, you know, 14,000 votes in Atlanta's Fulton County basically have the same impact as 132 votes in Chattahoochee County.

ANDERSON: Yes!

THOMPSON: Right.

KRUSE: And so politicians can campaign solely in these rural areas, because the rural counties, which have about a third of the state's population, have the majority of the county-unit votes. So you could campaign for statewide office in Georgia—and they did!—and never once setting foot in Atlanta, or Augusta, or Savannah, and simply hitting all these rural counties and racking up these votes from a small number of whites scattered in these rural segregationist areas. And so the politics reflect that, right?

ANDERSON: Mmhmm.

KRUSE: And so when the county-unit system comes before the Supreme Court in *Gray v. Sanders* in 1963, Justice William O. Douglas issues an 8–1 decision in which says basically the heart of democracy is one person, one vote, right? And so that's where we get the phrase, but it comes out of these internal battles inside the state over how state government is formed, how the counties have different powers, how it's spread out, and how it needs to be constantly updated and checked. So now, with *Shelby County v. Holder*, which is the Shelby County in Alabama, we've moved far away from that vital principle. The government has absented itself from these state politics, and I think with disastrous effects.

ANDERSON: Absolutely, absolutely.

DOWNS: All right, we have time for these two questions from the floor, so Anne first, then Catherine.

ANNE KORNHAUSER: Thank you. So I'm going to give a historical preface to it. I think it's a strategic question, a political question. I wonder if on the issue of voter suppression and the larger issue of democracy and ours not functioning too well if you could, one of the things history can tell us is, it's not one party or the other, right?

KRUSE: Yup.

ANNE: Because I think one of the big arguments . . . one of the big pushback arguments is "oh this is just a way to get more Democrats elected," because, you know, turnout helps Democrats, so I wonder what your thoughts are on that.

KRUSE: Well, I think we can stress the history of this. Again, if we tell the story of *Baker v. Carr*, it's a suburban Republican who brings the case. It's a white guy from suburban Shelby County who's upset that the suburbs are being ignored. But today, the roles are reversed, and for the last several decades, it's been Republicans who are now seeking to limit the vote. We often say, well, we don't have the smoking gun for this or that; but in this instance we kind of do. Conservative organizer Paul Weyrich in 1980 at the famous Religious Roundtable rally says, "A lot of these Christians have what I call the goo-goo syndrome: good government. They want everybody to vote. Well, I don't want everyone to vote." He says it quite explicitly, "Our leverage in the elections quite candidly goes up as the voting populace goes down." So that's a road map that's been there from the start of the Reagan era, and we've seen similar admissions every now and then. In the run-up to the 2012 election, the Republican leader in the Pennsylvania state House bragged about passing new requirements for voter identification at the polls, which, he said, "is going to allow Governor Romney to win the state of Pennsylvania."

THOMPSON: Right.

ANDERSON: Right.

KRUSE: So there have been these moments where the game does get exposed.

RICHARDSON: Well, that's . . . go ahead.

ABRAMS: Nope, you.

RICHARDSON: That's the present, though. The shoe was on the other foot in the nineteenth century.

KRUSE: Mmhmm.

RICHARDSON: This is about democracy; it's not about party.

ABRAMS: And the way I would articulate that is that in Georgia, we did a Super Bowl ad through Fair Fight Action, our organization, and it was a Republican county commissioner and I. Because they have held the same election for the Republican primary twice already in that county, and it had to be thrown out a second time, he gets a third election this month. Because the incompetence and malfeasance of voter suppression may be targeted at a certain community, but it can eviscerate democracy for everyone.

ANDERSON: Yes.

ABRAMS: That's the challenge—that while it may be the architecture of a certain party, when you corrode democracy, everything falls apart. In a county with six thousand voters who are participating in a primary, to have to run the same election three times because of the incompetence and the mismanagement of the voting process, the secretary of state and the counties were complicit in denying the right to vote. And I think we found about two thousand Democrats in that whole county.

[Chuckling]

ABRAMS: The rest of them were Republicans, so I do think that it is important for us to always articulate that while the targets may be largely African American, largely people of color, but include single white women, who face some of the same class challenges, and let's not forget college students, who are often the first targets of voter ID laws.

KRUSE AND THOMPSON: Right.

ANDERSON: Mmhmm.

ABRAMS: That there is nothing partisan about eliminating our democracy.

THOMPSON: But if I'm also hearing a little bit of what you're saying as well [gesturing to Anne Kornhauser], there can also be a fetishization of the Democratic Party as the savior party in this, because, of course, at every step along this historical path, the Democrats have many times been—and I'm not talking about the Dixiecrats here; I'm talking about the modern-day Democrats—have been intensely interested in disfranchising poor, urban, black voters too. So, I mean, exempting yourself from the democracy is often, at least it is in my city, "Who's representing me? Democrats aren't representing me. Republicans aren't representing me." And that's why the Obama moment is so interesting, because there is this kind of feeling of "maybe we'll be represented," but then deep dissatisfaction with the limitations of party politics. So I think that is an important thing, not partisanship, but in fact the democracy itself, however that may play out.

DOWNS: All right. And our final question from Catherine Clinton, the co-series editor of History in the Headlines.

CLINTON: Thank you.

THOMPSON: Happy birthday.

PARTICIPANTS: Happy birthday!

CLINTON: But what a great birthday present, to have this incredible conversation, so I just wanted to add something in. We're talking party politics, and of course Brexit is very much on my mind and what party politics can do to a democracy, and since I lived and taught in Northern Ireland for ten years, I'm thinking about how one does advance and not break down into party politics but talks about the enterprise of peace and prosperity and people living in families and people believing in government. So I moved to a state, Texas, where there is a new voter. There's a new population. It's younger; it's browner; it's going to change the state. What are we going to do?" And we see, immediately, these forces. So I'm asking really as a historian, much like Heather Cox Richardson, who concentrates on writing on the nineteenth century, and bringing the black voices out that matter in the twenty-first century is important, but what can we do now as spokespeople and historians to point out that there is, arresting people for voting, and deporting them, there certainly is the scare tactics. I register people in my college classroom, and then they go out and stand outside city hall to help people who are turned away. So how do we actively get the word out, in 2020, coming up? That's my question.

DOWNS: Great.

ANDERSON: Well, I—oh. [Turns to Abrams] Expert.

ABRAMS: Well, I don't have a "Dr." in front of my name.

[Laughter]

ABRAMS: Oh, Yale.

[More laughter]

THOMPSON: You have a juris doctorate.

ANDERSON: I would say that one of the key pieces is that we don't relax. We don't relax after 2018, right? After the midterms. And that we continue to engage, and that is critical. I mean, when I'm out and about, I don't have it on now, but when I'm on the plane or when I'm traveling, I have my button on, going, "I will vote." And it's just a signal. It's just a signal, and I see people looking. When I'm in the beauty shop, I'm talking about the issues. Again, one of the things that they did in Alabama is exactly what you talked about, was they didn't talk about the politicians—they talked about the issues. And so when I'm in the beauty shop, I'm listening to what folks are saying about their issues, and then we're talking about the issues, because of that kind of ongoing engagement in the issues. And then they're talking to their friends and then they're talking to their families—I mean it is this kind of network that's out there. When we're on social media, we're talking about it. When we're writing op-eds, we're talking about it. And it is that engagement. It means that we're not . . . we're not sitting back and waiting until June or October of 2020 to engage. We're staying engaged, and we're paying attention to the laws that are happening. And I have to tell you, I love the engagement that I'm seeing. When I'm seeing people calling their representatives to question a bill that is before the House, when I see them going to town halls, it is that engagement that's going to keep us moving forward. And it is . . . and it is, frankly, providing, when we can, funding to civil society to continue doing what I call that heavy lifting of democracy. So it is the ACLU and the League of Women Voters and the LDF because they are doing—and I give to Fair Fight every month, it's automatic. It is *automatic*. I'm telling you, your speech, it was like "yes!" And it's like, "Send, submit!"

[Laughter]

ANDERSON: And so it is knowing that there are these organizations that are continuing to do the work between the elections that's going to be absolutely essential in getting us the democracy that we deserve. So to me that's it—it is continuing to have the conversations, and I say . . . like when I'm talking about in *White Rage*, if Crazy Uncle Joe says something crazy, this is the time to educate Crazy Uncle Joe. Because everybody is sitting around the table listening to Crazy Uncle Joe, but they might not know it's really crazy. And you got to . . . "Well, you know Nixon just conceded."

KRUSE: Right.

ANDERSON: "He did it right, that really showed . . ."

KRUSE: Character.

ANDERSON: Well, I believe your line on Twitter, "Let's dig in."

KRUSE: Let's dig in.

[Laughter]

ABRAMS: The only thing I would add is that you all have an extraordinary network as historians, a network of students, of adjutants, but also a network of knowledge. And it's using that knowledge to not only push your own students but also talk to other historians to ensure that they are doing the same with their students.

PARTICIPANTS: Mmhmm.

ABRAMS: We tend to wait for organizations to come and ask for help, as opposed to recognizing that we are organizations ourselves and we can provide the help we're looking for. And so leveraging and sharing the same data points and saying, "Here's what we're doing. Are you doing that?" Because within this room is the ability to animate and activate thousands and thousands of not only young people but their parents and their friends. The information that you possess, the ability to respond not only on Twitter but to write a letter to the editor when you hear crazy . . .

KRUSE: Mmhmm.

ABRAMS: Or worse, when you hear something that sounds vaguely smart but is off by two degrees of knowledge.

KRUSE: Yep.

[Laughter]

ABRAMS: Those moments of intercession from historians is transformative because you not only tell the audience but you also give folks like myself who are repeating the bad information because it sounds like truth, you give us a better handle on what we should be saying and how we can contextualize. We need your help, and we want to know—I'm using the royal "we"—but for many of us the goal is to be able tell the story that people can hear, and there is nothing more provocative than being able to say, "This is what's happened. This is how it changed. And if you do this with me, this is what happens for you." And so you're also arming us with the information we need to be better at what we do.

RICHARDSON: You know I would also add that I think the people at this table have done exceedingly well, especially Kevin, and I always tell people, "Take up oxygen." Just whether you're a historian or somebody on the street . . . your crazy uncle's not going anywhere . . .

KRUSE: Right.

RICHARDSON: But your not-so-maybe-crazy cousin might be ready to hear something, and that's what you do so well on Twitter.

ANDERSON: Yup.

THOMPSON: Mmhmm.

RICHARDSON: So take up oxygen. But also I say to people these times are wearing a lot of people down *hard*.

ANDERSON: Whoo.

RICHARDSON: Sometimes just getting out of bed and going to work and putting in a day is an act of resistance, saying, "You are *not* going to get me this time. I'm going to file this report if it kills me," and going home. I think those moments of just getting out of bed, and even if you don't take up oxygen that day, are good enough. But if you can, take up oxygen.

DOWNS: Well, thank you so much, this has been so fun!

PARTICIPANTS: Thank you!

[Applause]

Top Ten Articles

Many of the topics covered in the roundtable are highlighted in the opinion pieces that follow. The "top ten" selection herein is by no means scientific nor definitive. The bibliography includes further resources regarding this topic, as does the series website for History in the Headlines (www.ugapress.org/index.php/series /HIH/).

Voter Suppression, Then and Now

DAVID W. BLIGHT

New York Times, September 7, 2012

Suppressing the black vote is a very old story in America, and it has never been just a southern thing.

In 1840, and again in 1841, the former Frederick Bailey, now Frederick Douglass, walked a few blocks from his rented apartment on Ray Street in New Bedford, Massachusetts, to the town hall, where he paid a local tax of $1.50 to register to vote. Born a slave on Maryland's Eastern Shore in 1818, Douglass escaped in an epic journey on trains and ferryboats, first to New York City, and then to the whaling port of New Bedford in 1838.

By the mid-1840s, he had emerged as one of the greatest orators and writers in American history. But legally, Douglass began his public life by committing what today we would consider voter fraud, using an assumed name.

It was a necessary step: when he registered to vote under his new identity, "Douglass," a name he took from Sir Walter Scott's 1810 epic poem "Lady of the Lake," this fugitive slave was effectively an illegal immigrant in Massachusetts. He was still the legal "property" of Thomas Auld, his owner in St. Michaels, Maryland, and susceptible, under the federal fugitive slave law, to capture and return to slavery at any time.

It was a risky move. If required, the only identification Douglass could give the registrar may have been his address in the town directory. He possessed two pieces of paper, which would only have endangered him more. One was a fraudulent "Seaman's Protection Paper," which he had borrowed in Baltimore from a retired free black sailor named Stanley, who was willing to support the young man's escape.

The second was a brief three-line certification of his marriage to Anna Murray, his free black fiancée, who joined him in New York just after his escape. A black minister, James Pennington, himself a former fugitive slave, married them, but on the document he called them Mr. and Mrs. "Johnson." Douglass was at least the fourth name Frederick had used to distract the authorities on his quest for freedom. He once remarked that a fugitive slave had to adopt various names to survive because "among honest men an honest man may well be content with one name . . . but toward fugitives, Americans are not honest."

Should this fugitive, who had committed the crime of stealing his own freedom and living under false identities, have been allowed to vote? Voting reforms in recent decades had broadened the franchise to include men who did not hold property but certainly not to anyone who was property.

Fortunately for Douglass, at the time Massachusetts was one of only five northern states that allowed suffrage for "free" blacks (the others were Vermont, Maine, New Hampshire, and Rhode Island).

Blacks in many other states weren't so lucky. Aside from Maine, every state that entered the Union after 1819 excluded them from voting. Four northern states—New York, Ohio, Indiana, and Wisconsin—had reaffirmed earlier black voter exclusion laws by the early 1850s. A few blacks actually voted in New York, but only if they could pass a stiff property qualification. The sheer depth of racism at the base of this story is remarkable, since in no northern state at the time, except New Jersey, did blacks constitute more than 2 percent of the population.

We do not know when Douglass cast his first vote. It might have been in 1840, in the famous "log cabin and hard cider" campaign mounted by the Whig Party for its candidate, General William Henry Harrison. If so, he likely supported the Liberty Party's James G. Birney, who represented the first genuinely antislavery party, however small, in American history; it achieved some strength in the Bay State.

In 1848 he spoke at the national convention of the newly formed Free Soil Party, and after 1854, haltingly at first and later wholeheartedly, he joined and worked for the new antislavery coalition known as the Republican Party, which ran and elected Abraham Lincoln in 1860. To this day, that "Grand Old Party" still calls itself the "party of Lincoln" and still claims Frederick Douglass as one of its black founders.

And indeed Douglass saw himself as a founder of that party, but only many years after a group of English antislavery friends purchased his freedom in 1846 for £150 ($711 at the time in American dollars). Douglass was in the midst of a triumphal two-year speaking tour of Ireland, Scotland, and England; when he returned to America in 1847, he moved to New York in possession of his official "manumission papers." He was free and legal, eventually owned property, and could vote. Valued and purchased as a commodity, he could now claim to be a citizen.

In Douglass's greatest speech, the Fourth of July oration in 1852, he argued that often the only way to describe American hypocrisy about race was with "scorching irony," "biting ridicule," and "withering sarcasm." Today's Republican Party seems deeply concerned with rooting out voter fraud of the kind Douglass practiced. So with Douglass's story as background, I have a modest proposal for it. In the twenty-three states where Republicans have either enacted voter ID laws or shortened early voting hours in urban districts, and consistent with their current reigning ideology, they should adopt a simpler strategy of voter suppression.

To those potentially millions of young, elderly, brown, and black registered voters who, despite no evidence of voter fraud, they now insist must obtain government ID, why not merely offer money? Pay them not to vote. Give each a check for $711 in honor of Frederick Douglass. Buy their "freedom," and the election. Call it the "Frederick Douglass Voter Voucher."

Give people a choice: take the money and just not vote, or travel miles without easy transportation to obtain a driver's license they do not need. It's their "liberty"; let them decide how best to use it. Perhaps they will forget their history as much as the Republican Party seems to wish the nation would.

Such an offer would be only a marginal expense for a "super PAC"—plus a bit more to cover the lawyers needed to prove it legal under federal election law—and no one would have to know who paid for this generous effort to stop fraud. Once and for all, the right can honestly declare what the Supreme Court has allowed it to practice: that voters are commodities, not citizens.

And, if the Republican Party wins the election in November, this plan will give it a splendid backdrop for next year's commemoration of the 150th anniversary of its great founder's Emancipation Proclamation.

How Prisons Change the Balance of Power in America

HEATHER ANN THOMPSON

The Atlantic, October 7, 2013

What has it really cost the United States to build the world's most massive prison system?

To answer this question, some point to the nearly two million people who are now locked up in an American prison—overwhelmingly this nation's poorest, most mentally ill, and least-educated citizens—and ponder the moral costs. Others have pointed to the enormous expense of having more than seven million Americans under some form of correctional supervision and argued that the system is not economically sustainable. Still others highlight the high price that our nation's already most-fragile communities, in particular, have paid for the rise of such an enormous carceral state. A few have also asked Americans to consider what it means for the future of our society that our system of punishment is so deeply racialized.

With so many powerful arguments being made against our current criminal-justice system, why then does it persist? Why haven't the American people, particularly those who are most negatively affected by this most unsettling and unsavory state of affairs, undone the policies that have led us here? The answer, in part, stems from the fact that locking up unprecedented numbers of citizens over the last forty years has *itself* made the prison system highly resistant to reform through the democratic process. To an extent that few Americans have yet appreciated, record rates of incarceration have, in fact, undermined our American democracy, both by impacting who gets to vote and how votes are counted.

The unsettling story of how this came to be actually begins in 1865, when the abolition of slavery led to bitter constitutional battles over who would and would not be included in our polity. To fully understand it, though, we must look more closely than we yet have at the year 1965, a century later—a moment when, on the one hand, politicians were pressured into opening the franchise by passing the most comprehensive Voting Rights Act to date, but on the other hand, were also beginning a devastatingly ambitious War on Crime.

FROM VOTING RIGHTS TO THE WAR ON CRIME

The Voting Rights Act of 1965 gave the federal government a number of meaningful tools with which it could monitor state elections and make sure that states with a particularly grim history of discriminatory voting practices would make no voting policy without its approval. The act had been intended to combat the intimidation and legal maneuvers—such as passage of poll taxes, literacy requirements, and so-called "grandfather clauses"—that had left only 5 percent of black Americans, by the 1940s, able to vote, despite passage of the Fourteenth and Fifteenth Amendments after the Civil War.

But the very same year that Lyndon Johnson signed the Voting Rights Act of 1965, he also signed another act into law: the Law Enforcement Administration Act (LEAA), a piece of legislation that, well before crime rates across America hit record highs, created the bureaucracy and provided the funding that would enable a historically and internationally unparalleled war on crime.

So, at the *very same moment* that the American civil rights movement had succeeded in newly empowering African Americans in the political sphere by securing passage of the Voting Rights Act of 1965, America's white politicians decided to begin a massive new war on crime that would eventually undercut myriad gains of the civil rights movement—*particularly* those promised by the Voting Rights Act itself.

FROM THE WAR ON CRIME TO MASS INCARCERATION

Thanks to LEAA and America's post-1965 commitment to the War on Crime, and more specifically, thanks to the dramatic escalation of policing in cities across the nation as well as the legal changes wrought by an ever-intensifying War on Drugs, between 1970 and 2010 more people ended up in prison in this country than anywhere else in the world. At no other point in this nation's recorded past had the economic, social, and political institutions of a country become so bound up with the practice of punishment.

By the year 2007, one in every thirty-one U.S. residents lived under some form of correctional supervision. By 2010, more than 7.3 million Americans had become entangled in the criminal-justice system and two million of them were actually locked up in state and federal prisons. By 2011, 39,709 people in Louisiana alone were living behind bars and 71,579 were either in jail, on probation, or on parole. And this was by no means a "southern" phenomenon. In Pennsylvania, 51,638 people were actually locked behind bars in 2011 and a full 346,268 lived under some form of correctional control by that year.

The nation's decision to embark on a massive War on Crime in the mid-1960s has had a profound impact on the way that American history evolved over the course of the later twentieth and into the twenty-first centuries. As we now know from countless studies, such staggering rates of incarceration have proven both socially devastating and economically destructive for wide swaths of this country—particularly those areas of America inhabited by people of color. This nation's incarceration rate was hardly color-blind. Eventually one in nine young black men were locked up in America and, by 2010, black women and girls too were being locked up at a record rate.

DILUTING OUR DEMOCRACY

So how did this overwhelmingly racialized mass incarceration end up mattering to our very democracy? How is it that this act of locking up so many Americans, particularly Americans of color, *itself* distorted our political process and made it almost impossible for those most affected by mass incarceration to eliminate the policies that have undergirded it at the ballot box? The answer lies back in the 1870s and in a little-known caveat to the Fourteenth Amendment.

Ratifying the Fourteenth Amendment was one of Congress's first efforts to broaden the franchise after the Civil War. A key worry among northern politicians, however, was that since white southerners could no longer rely on the notorious "three-fifths" rule to pad their own political power, they would now try to inflate their census population for the purposes of representation by counting African Americans as citizens while denying them to access the ballot.

So, to prevent any power grab on the part of ex-Confederates, Congress decided to add so-called section 2 to the Fourteenth Amendment. Firstly it stipulated that any state that "denied" the vote "to any of the male inhabitants of such state, being twenty-one years of age, and citizens of the United States" would have its representation downsized in proportion to the number of individuals being disenfranchised. Secondly, section 2 allowed for the disenfranchisement of otherwise eligible citizens—without affecting representation—if they had participated "in rebellion, or other crime." The idea here was to keep those who had committed crimes against the Union and those who might still be in rebellion against the Union from wielding political power in the wake of the Civil War.

This latter provision of section 2, however, proved damaging to black freedom—political and otherwise. Almost overnight, white southerners began policing African Americans with new zeal and charging them with "crimes" that had never before been on the books. Within a decade of the Civil War, thousands of African Americans found themselves leased out and locked up on prison plantations and in penitentiaries.

Southern whites, of course, profited from these new laws politically as well as economically. By making so many blacks into convicts, whites could deny them the right to vote under section 2 without undermining their state's census population for the purposes of political representation. And, because of another clause of another amendment, the Thirteenth, which allowed the continuation of slavery for those who had committed a crime, these same white southerners were able to force thousands of newly imprisoned black southerners to work for free under the convict lease system.

Fast-forward one hundred years when, in the wake of the civil rights movement, another War on Crime began that also, almost overnight, led to the mass imprisonment of this nation's African American citizens.

In 1974, as the number of imprisoned Americans was rising precipitously and when states once again began to disfranchise individuals with criminal convictions, the U.S. Supreme Court was asked in a landmark case, *Richardson v. Ramirez*, to rule explicitly on the issue of whether it was constitutional under the Fourteenth Amendment to disfranchise those serving, or who have served, time in prison. The court did the same thing that many southern states did after the Civil War—it interpreted section A of the Fourteenth Amendment very, very differently than it was intended to be interpreted. It, too, decided that disenfranchisement would be permitted when a citizen was convicted of *any* crime, without regard to whether such crimes might be thought of as ideologically analogous to rebellion or were more likely to affect African Americans than others.

Notably, Justice Thurgood Marshall dissented vigorously in this case. The purpose of section 2, he argued, was clearly to enfranchise, not disenfranchise, former slaves and their descendants. Marshall's fellow members of the bench, though, felt that their decision would not have any discriminatory effect because the nation already had the Voting Rights Act of 1965 to handle this issue.

And yet, the negative impact of *Richardson v. Ramirez* on African American voting was vast and immediate. By the year 2000, 1.8 million African Americans had been barred from the polls because so many felon disfranchisement laws had been passed in states across the country after 1974. Not only were their votes not counted in that year's hotly contested presidential election, but by the next presidential election a full ten states, according to the Sentencing Project, had "African American disenfranchisement rates above 15%," which clearly affected the outcome of that contest as well.

By 2006, forty-eight out of fifty states had passed disfranchisement laws and, with more than forty-seven million Americans (one-fourth of the adult population) having criminal records by that year, the nation's political process had been fundamentally altered. By 2011, 23.3 percent of African Americans in Florida, 18.3 percent of the black population of Wyoming, and 20.4 percent of African Americans in Virginia were barred from the ballot.

According to sociologists Jeff Manza and Christopher Uggen, not only did African Americans pay a high price for the disfranchisement policies that accompanied the nation's War on Crime, but so did liberal voters in general. According to their research, such policies "affected the outcome of seven U.S. Senate races from 1970 to 1998 . . . [and] in each case the Democratic candidate would have won rather than the Republican victor" and these outcomes likely "prevented Democratic control of the Senate from 1986 to 2000" as well.

DISTORTING OUR DEMOCRACY

Disfranchising thousands of voters is only part of the story of how mass incarceration has distorted American democracy. Today, just as it did more than a hundred years earlier, the way the Census calculates resident population also plays a subtle but significant role. As ex-Confederates knew well, prisoners would be counted as residents of a given county, even if they could not themselves vote:

high numbers of prisoners could easily translate to greater political power for those who put them behind bars.

With the advent of mass incarceration, and as the number of people imprisoned not only rose dramatically but also began moving urbanites of color into overwhelmingly white rural counties that housed prisons, the political process was again distorted. In short, thanks to this process that we now call "prison gerrymandering," overwhelmingly white and Republican areas of the United States that built prisons as the War on Crime escalated got more political power, whereas areas of country where policing was particularly concentrated and aggressive, areas in which levels of incarceration were, as a result, staggering, lost political power.

Consider research by the Prison Policy Initiative showing how voters across the country gain political power from housing a penal facility. In Powhatan County, Virginia, 41 percent of the Fifth Board of Supervisors District that was drawn after the 2000 Census were actually people in prison and in both the First and Third Supervisory Districts of Nottoway County, approximately one-fourth of their population comes from large prisons within the county. In the case of Southampton County, such prison-based gerrymandering means that votes of those citizens who live there are worth almost more than twice as much as votes cast in other districts that have the required number of actual residents.

In Michigan as well, mass incarceration has meant distorted democracy. A full four state senate districts drawn after the 2000 Census (17, 19, 33, and 37), and a full five house districts (65, 70, 92, 107, and 110) meet federal minimum population requirements only because they claim prisoners as constituents. Similarly in Pennsylvania, no fewer than eight state legislative districts would comply with the federal "one person, one vote" civil rights standard if nonvoting state and federal prisoners in those districts were not counted as district residents.

WHY WE SHOULD CARE

As Americans go to the polls this November to vote on criminal-justice issues that directly affect our lives—ranging from proposals to decriminalize marijuana, to roll back three strikes laws, to fund more prison construction—the massive carceral state that we are trying to shape at the ballot box has already distorted our democracy. Americans' power to even rethink, let alone undo, the policies and practices that have led to mass incarceration via the franchise has been severely compromised—in no small part due to the fact that the parties that benefited the most from the rise of this enormous carceral state are now empowered, seemingly in perpetuity, by its sheer size and scope.

There are, of course, other ways to dismantle the carceral state. Indeed, history shows us that we ended the brutal convict-leasing system of the post–Civil War era not by going to the polls but by grassroots and legal activism. Nevertheless, we should all be concerned about the ways mass incarceration has eroded our democracy. Even if we don't care about the record rate of imprisonment in this country—despite its myriad ugly consequences, its unsustainable cost, and its particularly devastating fallout on communities of color—when the principle of "one person, one vote" no longer has real meaning in a society, and when political power is no longer attained via its people but rather through a manipulation of their laws, we must all question the future of our nation.

Why We Still Need the Voting Rights Act

JOHN LEWIS

Washington Post, February 24, 2013

On "Bloody Sunday," nearly fifty years ago, Hosea Williams and I led six hundred peaceful, nonviolent protesters attempting to march from Selma to Montgomery to dramatize the need for voting rights protection in Alabama. As we crossed the Edmund Pettus Bridge, we were attacked by state troopers who tear-gassed, clubbed, and whipped us and trampled us with horses. I was hit in the head with a nightstick and suffered a concussion on the bridge. Seventeen marchers were hospitalized that day.

In response, President Lyndon Johnson introduced the Voting Rights Act and later signed it into law. We have come a great distance since then, in large part thanks to the act, but efforts to undermine the voting power of minorities did not end after 1965. They still persist today.

This week the Supreme Court will hear one of the most important cases in our generation, *Shelby County v. Holder*. At issue is section 5 of the Voting Rights Act, which requires all or parts of sixteen "covered" states with long histories and contemporary records of voting discrimination to seek approval from the federal government for voting changes. The court is questioning whether section 5 remains a necessary remedy for ongoing discrimination.

In 2006, Congress debated this very question over ten months. We held twenty-one hearings, heard from more than ninety witnesses, and reviewed more than fifteen thousand pages of evidence. We analyzed voting patterns in and outside the sixteen covered jurisdictions. We considered four amendments on the floor of the House; the Senate Judiciary Committee considered several others.

After all of that, Congress came to a near-unanimous conclusion: While some change has occurred, the places with a legacy of longstanding, entrenched and state-sponsored voting discrimination still have the most persistent, flagrant, contemporary records of discrimination in this country. While the sixteen jurisdictions affected by section 5 represent only 25 percent of the nation's population, they still represent more than 80 percent of the lawsuits proving cases of voting discrimination.

It is ironic and almost emblematic that the worst perpetrators are those seeking to be relieved of the responsibilities of justice. Instead of accepting the ways our society has changed and dealing with the implications of true democracy, they would rather free themselves of oversight and the obligations of equal justice.

Calera, a city in Shelby County, Alabama, provides a prime example. Once it was an all-white suburb of Birmingham. Rapid growth created one majority-black district that in 2004 had the power, for the first time, to elect a candidate of its choice to city government, Ernest Montgomery.

Just before the 2008 election, however, the city legislature redrew the boundaries to include three white-majority districts in an effort to dilute the voting power of black citizens. The Justice Department blocked the plan, but Calera held the election anyway, and Montgomery was toppled from his seat.

In 2012, section 5 was used to block Texas from implementing the most restrictive voter law in the country, which threatened the rights of more than six hundred thousand registered voters, predominantly Latinos and African Americans.

Kilmichael, Mississippi, was blocked from canceling elections shortly after the results of the 2000 Census demonstrated a black-voting majority that could, for the first time, elect the candidate of its choice.

Such cases are numerous and exemplify the "unprecedented legislative record" amassed in 2006. That mountain of evidence paved the way for a bipartisan majority in Congress to reauthorize section 5 by a vote of 390 to 33 in the House and 98 to 0 in the Senate.

Opponents of section 5 complain of state expense, yet their only cost is the paper, postage, and manpower required to send copies of legislation to the federal government for review, hardly a punishment.

But without section 5, guaranteed civil liberties of millions of voters could be flagrantly denied, and those violations would remain in force and nearly unchecked unless a lawsuit provided some eventual relief. The act also rewards progress. In fact, every jurisdiction that has applied for bailout, demonstrating a clean record over ten years, has been freed from section 5 compliance.

Evidence proves there are forces in this country that willfully and intentionally trample on the voting rights of millions of Americans. That is why every president and every Congress, regardless of politics or party, has reauthorized section 5.

The right to vote is the most powerful nonviolent tool we have in a democracy. I risked my life defending that right. Some died in the struggle. If we are ever to actualize the true meaning of equality, effective measures such as the Voting Rights Act are still a necessary requirement of democracy.

Why the Voting Rights Act Is Once Again under Threat

ARI BERMAN

New York Times, August 6, 2015

In his opinion for the majority in the Supreme Court's 2013 *Shelby County* decision, which struck down a major section of the Voting Rights Act, Chief Justice John G. Roberts Jr. wrote that "history did not end in 1965." But the sad truth is that voter-suppression efforts did not end, either.

In 2014, the first post-*Shelby* election, thousands were turned away by new restrictions in states like Texas and North Carolina. A 2014 study by the Government Accountability Office found that voter ID laws in Kansas and Tennessee reduced turnout by 2 to 3 percent during the 2012 election, enough to swing a close vote, with the highest drop-off among young, black, and newly registered voters.

This could be a disturbing preview for 2016, which will be the first presidential contest in fifty years where voters cannot rely on the full protections of the act. New restrictions will be in place in up to fifteen states, which account for as many as 162 electoral votes, including crucial swing states like Ohio, Wisconsin, and Virginia.

The act, signed fifty years ago today, was the crowning achievement of the civil rights movement. It swept aside longstanding practices that disenfranchised voters and prevented new ones from emerging: between 1965 and 2013 the Justice Department and federal courts blocked more than three thousand discriminatory voting changes. But it is precisely that capacity, known as preclearance, that the Roberts court invalidated.

The backlash to the law was as immediate as its progress. Southern states quickly challenged its constitutionality, and several changed their election laws to stop newly registered black voters and candidates from winning elected office.

The battle soon shifted from registration to representation, from the right to vote to the value of that vote. In 1969, the Supreme Court declared that the federal government had the power to block the "second-generation" voting restrictions adopted by southern states to subvert the growing minority vote, like gerrymandering, consolidating smaller black areas with larger white ones, and switching from district to countywide elections, where the white majority remained in control.

But as the reach of the law expanded, so did the opposition to it. When minority candidates began to be elected in large numbers in the 1970s and 1980s, "colorblindness" replaced states' rights as a more respectable rallying cry for opponents. They held that the law should only block obstacles to voter registration, like literacy tests, rather than outlawing electoral schemes that prevented minority voters from winning office.

In the 1980s, resistance to the civil rights laws of the 1960s became a defining cause for ambitious young conservatives like John Roberts, who wrote dozens of memos criticizing the Voting Rights Act while serving in the Reagan Justice Department. He believed the act should prohibit only intentional discrimination in voting, which was nearly impossible to prove. He lost that fight when Congress overwhelmingly reauthorized the act in 1982, but the Reagan administration appointed a generation of judges who approached it with deep skepticism.

The backlash entered a new phase after the 2000 election, when a botched voter purge in Florida, while Jeb Bush was governor, disproportionately prevented African Americans from voting and helped George W. Bush win the White House. The Bush administration reoriented the Justice Department, prioritizing prosecutions of voter fraud over investigations into voter disenfranchisement.

The push to make it harder to vote escalated after the Tea Party's triumph in the 2010 elections, when half the states, nearly all of them under Republican control, passed new voting restrictions, which disproportionately targeted the core of President Obama's coalition, particularly minority voters. The voting changes were subtler than those of the 1960s, camouflaging efforts to deter voting with laws that rarely invoked race, introduced with equal fervor in North and South alike.

Many of these laws were blocked in court during the 2012 election and helped inspire a backlash by minority voters. That year, for the first time in a presidential election, the percentage of blacks who turned out to vote exceeded that of whites.

Then came *Shelby County*. Laws that were previously stopped under the act, like Texas's strict voter ID law, immediately went into effect, while new states rushed to pass tougher voting restrictions. (On Wednesday the Fifth Circuit Court of Appeals largely upheld a lower-court ruling that struck down the Texas law.) A month after the *Shelby County* decision, North Carolina passed a sweeping restructuring of its election system, repealing or curtailing nearly every reform in the state that made it easier to vote.

The Justice Department and civil rights groups are challenging the new law in federal court. North Carolina is making the familiar argument that the lawsuit amounts to "the equivalent of election law affirmative action."

But even if the plaintiffs win, that's just one law, in one state. The voting rights landscape today most closely resembles the period before 1965, when the blight of voting discrimination could be challenged only on a torturous case-by-case basis.

What can be done? The Voting Rights Advancement Act of 2015, introduced in Congress in June, would compel states with a recent history of voting discrimination to once again clear election changes with the federal government and would require approval for specific measures that often target minority voters today. But the bill hasn't gone anywhere. On the fiftieth anniversary of the Voting Rights Act, Congress won't even schedule a hearing.

The Long and Despicable Roots of Voter Suppression and Similar Tactics

FRANK PALMERI AND TED WENDELIN

History News Network, April 22, 2018

The South may have lost the Civil War militarily, but it won politically. For most of U.S. history, laws and policies that favor the South have prevailed. Originally, this hegemony was based on the southern states' paradoxical use of slavery to seize disproportionate power in national institutions. At the beginning of the Republic, slave states wanted to count each slave as one person for the purpose of apportioning representatives in the House. However, slaves had no civil rights, couldn't vote, and would not in fact be represented by those elected on this basis; the North therefore took the position that slaves should not be counted as part of the population. As a compromise, the Constitution established that each slave counted as three-fifths of a person. This compromise in effect gave the southern states a third more seats in Congress, and a third more electoral votes, than if slaves had not been counted as persons.

The three-fifths rule guaranteed the dominance of southern or slaveholder interests not only through the antebellum period but also thereafter through a long series of laws, practices, and Supreme

Court decisions. For example, the Missouri Compromise in 1820 preserved the constitutional compromise, and southern ascendancy, by resolving that for each free state admitted into the Union, a slave state would also be admitted.

To prevent even any discussion of slavery from 1836 to 1844, the House of Representatives passed gag rules in the form of resolutions that tabled without discussion any antislavery petition. The Missouri Compromise was overturned by the Compromise of 1850, a body of laws that included the Fugitive Slave Act, which required citizens to assist in the recapture of escaped slaves. Further, in 1854, the Kansas-Nebraska Act left the decision of slave or free up to the territory applying for statehood, but resulted in battles between partisans of the two sides, as in Bloody Kansas, for example.

Of course, during the Civil War and Reconstruction, the South did not dominate national politics. However, as soon as the last federal troops were withdrawn from the states of the Confederacy in 1877, the South developed new techniques for ensuring the disproportionate power of southern white voters. Through murder, intimidation, and fraud, the former slave states disenfranchised their black citizens while using them to obtain a number of representatives in Congress and the Electoral College based on total population in those states, including that black population. The South thus carried over the effects of the three-fifths rule through the post–Civil War period of the nineteenth century and at least the first two-thirds of the twentieth century.

By the 1890s, southern politicians had succeeded in imposing a legal regime of racial apartheid. Repeatedly reelected by white voters in one-party states, southern Democrats through their seniority controlled numerous chairmanships on important committees in Congress, giving them control over budgets, rules, and patronage projects. Their power enabled them to block federal legislation against lynching and other abuses in the South.

The racial segregation of public schools, transportation, hotels, restaurants, restrooms, and drinking fountains, based on separate but supposedly equal accommodation of the races, was affirmed by the Supreme Court in *Plessy v. Ferguson* in 1896. This system for depriving blacks of their civil rights persisted for more than seventy years, until the effects of the civil rights legislation of the mid-1960s began to be felt.

Even the progressive reforms of New Deal legislation in the 1930s excluded African Americans from most benefits and protections. Since southern Democrats were needed to pass any bill, Congress explicitly excluded occupations in which African Americans were strongly overrepresented, such as maids and farmworkers, from receiving Social Security benefits and worker protections such as minimum wage laws and the right to join unions. In addition, these laws were administered by local officials who were often ill-disposed toward African Americans, and southern Democrats prevented Congress from attaching antidiscrimination provisions to social-welfare programs.

Similarly, the practice of redlining developed by the Federal Housing Authority denied or limited mortgages and other financial services to neighborhoods based on racial composition. Redlining reduced the African American rate of homeownership, home values, and credit scores. In underdeveloped neighborhoods that local banks deemed unfit for investment because of redlining, African Americans' access to banking, retail merchandise, and even groceries was and has continued to be severely limited.

The lack of financing that prevented most African Americans from buying homes limited their ability to leave their heirs an estate. Because inheritance is the principal driver for the acquisition of wealth in the United States, African Americans have thus been hamstrung for generations in the pursuit of the American Dream.

The only other time the South was unable to exert effective control over national political life, apart from the Civil War and Reconstruction, was during a period of about a decade beginning in the mid-late 1960s. The Civil Rights Act of 1964 and the Voting Rights Act of 1965 exemplify legislative accomplishments of this time that pulled the South into the twentieth century. The Fair Housing Act of 1968 outlawed redlining, but the damage had been done and could not be easily reversed.

Southern hegemony returned with the electoral "southern strategy" pursued by Richard Nixon and subsequent Republican national candidates. The seventies saw a mass exodus of southern whites and southern politicians from the Democratic Party to the Republican Party, and that party moved further and further to the right, refining its use of racial codewords to appeal to white voters centrally but not exclusively in the South. The Republican National Committee admitted the strategy of exploiting racial antagonisms and apologized for it to the NAACP in 2005; yet the party still pursues this path energetically, and the current Republican president has attracted and not disavowed the enthusiastic support of neo-Nazis and former Klan members in the South and in other regions.

Taking advantage of the elimination of crucial preclearance requirements in the Voting Rights Act by *Shelby County v. Holder* in 2013, current strategies for disenfranchising African Americans, college students, and the poor echo earlier Jim Crow, segregationist voter-suppression tactics such as poll taxes, reading tests, and grandfather clauses. These practices include racially biased gerry-mandering, extreme voter-identification requirements, and use of the notorious Cross-Check system which allows state officials to purge from the rolls eligible voters who have the same minority-sounding names as others in different states, on the absurd theory that they may be the same person voting twice in the same election.

Thus, the instruments of racial oppression developed in the South continue to be employed today. Like wealthy slaveholders and their apologists, members of the far right today—and this includes a large majority of the Republican Party—share methods, language, and values that promote undemocratic results. They condemn the supposed tyranny of the federal government and feel themselves to be its innocent victims. As part of their plan to pursue small government and privatize enormous parts of public services, which the wealthiest among them will buy, control, and profit from, they attack public education and attempt to deprive working people of retirement benefits, unions, healthcare, and safety and environmental protections.

The conviction by far-right Christians in the Bible Belt (and elsewhere) of their own righteousness arose in the post–Civil War era, when politicians who wanted to expel federal troops and force out African American officeholders came to call themselves Redeemer Democrats. White southerners appropriated the term from Christian theology to describe the political transformation they desired.

Thus, the disproportionate representation in the national government granted to the South by the three-fifths rule in the Constitution was reestablished after the Civil War through voter suppression, backed up by terror, violence, and intimidation with the sanction of religion. As a result of the continuing dominance of the South, the social-welfare legislation of the New Deal applied almost exclusively to whites. Moreover, after the civil rights legislation of the 1960s, reactionary forces centered in and led by the South sought ways to evade or undermine these laws, beginning in the administration of Ronald Reagan, and continuing with increasing success in those of George W. Bush and Donald Trump.

For example, in 1981–82, as a conservative young lawyer in Reagan's Justice Department, John Roberts crusaded against congressional renewal of the preclearance section in the Voting Rights Act. Thirty years later, as chief justice, he wrote the *Shelby* decision that invalidated that section and gutted the law. Roberts argued that preclearance violated the "equal sovereignty of the states," a concept not found in the Constitution, but one which was used by Chief Justice Roger Taney as grounds for the notorious *Dred Scott* decision of 1857.

The results of the Civil Rights Act and the Voting Rights Act dragged an unwilling South into the twentieth century. In subsequent years the Republican Party, with its foundation now in the solid South, has done all it can to drag the country back into the nineteenth century through egregious voter suppression, mass incarceration, and financial and economic deprivation—actions that are no longer limited to the South, but which manifest themselves in other regions of the United States as well. The intransigence of the South and its allies renders the future of the country contentious and bleak.

The Republican Approach to Voter Fraud: Lie

CAROL ANDERSON

New York Times, September 8, 2018

He was a proud Korean War veteran. He was also black and lived in Texas. That meant that by 2013, Floyd Carrier, eighty-six, was a prime target for the state's voter-suppression campaign, even though he was "army strong."

In an election that year, when he handed his Department of Veterans Affairs card to the registrar, he was turned away. No matter that he had used that ID for more than fifty years without a problem. Texas had recently passed a burdensome and unnecessary law that required voters to show a state-approved ID with a photo. His card didn't have one.

The North Koreans couldn't break Mr. Carrier, but voter suppression did. "I wasn't a citizen no more," he told a reporter last year. "I wasn't."

Voters across the country are now realizing that they, too, have crossed into the twilight zone: citizens of America without full citizenship rights. The right to vote is central to American democracy. "It's preservative of all rights," as the Supreme Court said in its 1886 ruling in *Yick Wo v. Hopkins*. But chipping away at access to that right has been a central electoral strategy for Republicans.

Anthony Settles, a Texas retiree, had been repeatedly blocked from the ballot box because his mother changed his last name when he was a teenager, and that fifty-year-old paperwork was lost in what he described as a "bureaucratic nightmare." After spending months looking for the wayward document, and then trying to get certified by the name he has used for more than half a century, he knew, beyond all doubt, that he had been targeted.

"The intent of this law is to suppress the vote," Mr. Settles told a *Washington Post* reporter in 2016. "I feel like I'm not wanted in this state."

That was the point. Demoralize people. Strip away their voting rights. Debase their citizenship. Dilute the diversity of voters until the electorate becomes homogeneous. Lie and say it's because of voter fraud. But most important, do all of this in the name of saving democracy.

Rampant voter fraud does not exist. There is no epidemic of illegal voting. But the lie is so mesmerizing, it takes off like a wildfire so that the irrational fear that someone might vote who shouldn't means that hundreds of thousands who should can't cast ballots, in part because of the increase in voter ID laws across the country in recent years.

The best way to understand the lie is to understand how it began: on election day in 2000. What happened then affects who will show up to vote in less than two months, and how confident they'll feel when they get to the polls.

Florida's electoral malfeasance in the 2000 vote is infamous. But that election in St. Louis was also a disaster, and it taught the Republicans an important lesson: Block people of color from polling places by any means necessary. And it showed them, point by point, how to create a voter-suppression road map that is paying dividends today.

The St. Louis Board of Elections had purged some fifty thousand names from the voter rolls, primarily in key Democratic precincts.

And it had failed to notify the people who had just been stripped of their vote, as the law required.

So when those voters showed up to cast their ballots, they were told they were no longer registered. Besieged precinct workers couldn't get through on the jammed phone lines to check much of anything. Some opted to send frustrated would-be voters downtown to the Board of Elections office to resolve the issue there.

This combination of poor record keeping and ill-prepared officials meant that hours and hours dissolved as the clock on election day wound down. When the polls were about to close, the lobby was still packed with people waiting to cast their ballots.

Democrats filed for an injunction to keep precincts open to accommodate voters who had been caught in the Board of Elections runaround. A circuit court judge agreed and ordered the polls to stay open for a few more hours.

Republicans were not having it. Senator Christopher Bond said the voting extension "represents the biggest fraud on the voters in this state and nation that we have ever seen." Others made the case that this was just a Democratic maneuver that would result in hundreds of fraudulent votes.

Republicans filed an appeal to close the polls. A state appeals court obliged. Shortly after the circuit court's decision, the doors slammed shut on hundreds of people waiting in lines to vote.

Then things got worse.

Missouri Republicans twisted this clear case of election board wrongdoing into a torrent of accusations against the Democrats and the overwhelmingly black residents of St. Louis. Missouri's Republican secretary of state, Matt Blunt, called the effort to keep the polls open an attempt "to create bedlam so that election fraud could be perpetrated." Senator Bond went further: It was a "brazen" and "shocking" effort to commit voter fraud.

It was, of course, nothing of the sort. Instead, it was an illegitimate purge of approximately 49,589 eligible voters by the Board of Elections. It was also sloppy record keeping and bureaucratic malfeasance. But, for the Republicans, that was not the point. Rather, it was about fine-tuning a voter-suppression master plan. They learned three key lessons from the bungled election.

The first lesson was that demographics were not destiny. The voting-age population was becoming less white and more African American, Latino, and Asian. In 1992, nonwhite voters made up 13 percent of the American electorate. By 2012 that figure had risen to 28 percent. That growing share of the electorate favored the Democrats. A poll by the Joint Center for Political and Economic Studies in the late 1980s found that only one in two black Republicans thought his party cared about problems facing the black community. In the 2000 presidential election, nine in ten black voters, 62 percent of Hispanic voters, and just over half of all Asian voters backed Al Gore.

The Republicans' response to this? Block people of color from the ballot box. Consider the brutal clarity of Paul Weyrich, a founder of the Heritage Foundation and the American Legislative Exchange Council, which eventually helped write voter-suppression legislation that spread like a cancer across the country: "I don't want everybody to vote," he said in a 1980 speech to conservative preachers in Dallas. "Our leverage in the elections, quite candidly, goes up as the voting populace goes down." The Republican Party learned that voter suppression, done ruthlessly and relentlessly, could deliver victory.

The second lesson was the importance of controlling the machinery that decided the rules for voting, the conditions upon which those votes would be cast, and whose vote counted and whose did not. In 2000, the Florida secretary of state, Katherine Harris, proved this point beyond all doubt. Ms. Harris, a delegate at the Republican National Convention that year and a cochairwoman of George W. Bush's Florida campaign, used her power to undermine the recount.

She was in good company. She had the full support of the presidential candidate's brother, Governor Jeb Bush, who surreptitiously sent in his fixer, the Republican lobbyist Mac Stipanovich, to keep the secretary of state focused.

The key was to override the state's law that identified "intent of the voter" as the "gold standard" for a manual recount in Florida. Was the hanging chad clear on the ballot but unreadable by the machine? Had the voter written in the preferred candidate's name instead of marking the oval? When some of the counties had volunteers hand-count a representative sample of the ballots, they focused on the voter's intent.

Ms. Harris and Mr. Stipanovich sent in an undercover ally, Kerey Carpenter, a lawyer, to give guidance to Palm Beach County's canvassing board. Al Gore was gaining ground fast, which could have prompted a full-blown recount. But Ms. Carpenter's supposedly unbiased legal advice tilted the scales. She raised the standard for "intent" so high that Mr. Gore's lead fell to only six votes at one point, according to David Margolick's reporting of the recount in *Vanity Fair*.

Then she persuaded the chairman of the canvassing board to get Ms. Harris's opinion on whether a full recount was even necessary. Of course, the preordained answer was no. The voting machines had to be completely broken, not simply malfunctioning, the secretary of state ruled. Then Ms. Harris moved up the deadline for when the manual count had to be completed, to a date well before two major counties, Palm Beach and Miami-Dade, had even decided whether to do a recount.

In one egregious case, the standards that determined which absentee ballots were valid and which were not varied. The most salient factor became the political tilt of the county. Republican-leaning counties got much more leeway in counting overseas ballots that were completed, but not necessarily postmarked, on election day.

As a result, George W. Bush, who lost the popular vote, carried Florida by 537 votes, won the Electoral College, and became the forty-third president with a key assist by the Supreme Court.

This win, unlike any other, showed Republicans that the people in control of the levers of the electoral and political machinery could give an aura of legality to wanton purges, bureaucratic run-arounds, and other chicanery.

The final and perhaps most important lesson from 2000 was to lie. Lie often. Say the lies loud; say them with pride. Lie over and over and over. Lie without shame. Lie until the truth is drowned out, dead. Lie until no amount of evidence could convince anyone otherwise. Lie until there is no other narrative.

Senator Bond seemed to learn this well. He repeatedly claimed that Democrats were using the names of dead people and dogs to vote. He insisted that other people were creating fake addresses at vacant lots. Just as the best lies hold a kernel of truth, Senator Bond chose wisely.

Some prankster had indeed registered a thirteen-year-old springer spaniel, Ritzy Meckler, to vote. Yet there is no record anywhere of Fido, Rover, Lassie, or even Ritzy casting a ballot. Similarly, the myth of a swarm of fraudulent voters using the addresses of vacant lots to tilt the election to the Democrats, while tantalizing, collapsed under scrutiny. An investigation found that the city had wrongly listed sixty-five of the seventy-nine suspicious addresses as vacant.

Senator Bond did eventually find a dead person on the voter registration rolls, a former city alderman. But there was no evidence that anyone with his name voted in the 2000 election. By the time all of Senator Bond's claims had been investigated, it was clear that out of the 2.3 million Missouri voters, four people committed some type of malfeasance—hardly constituting "brazen" voter fraud.

And it was also obvious that mandating a photo ID at the polls would not have prevented that. But Senator Bond's leadership on the Help America Vote Act, which was designed to solve the "problems" that emerged in the 2000 election, required that the lie of voter fraud and the need for voter ID become embedded in federal law.

Republicans had fashioned a noose around our democracy. And it's only getting tighter and tighter.

How Voter Suppression Could Swing the Midterms

ARI BERMAN

New York Times, October 27, 2018

In the weeks before an election, political campaigns are focused on getting voters to the polls—holding rallies, knocking on doors, and making phone calls to make sure people show up.

In Georgia and other states, the question in this election is not just about which candidates voters will support but whether they'll be able to cast a ballot in the first place. The fight over voting rights in the midterms is a reminder that elections are not solely about who is running, what their commercials say, or how many people are registered to vote. They are about who is allowed to vote and which officials are placing obstacles in the way of would-be voters.

The issue of voter suppression has exploded in recent weeks, most notably in the Georgia governor's race between Stacey Abrams, a Democrat, and Brian Kemp, a Republican. While running for higher office, Mr. Kemp, as secretary of state, also enforces Georgia's voting laws. This month, the Associated Press reported that Mr. Kemp's office had put more than fifty-three thousand voter registration applications in limbo because the information on the forms did not exactly match state databases. Seventy percent of the pending registrations were from African Americans, leading Ms. Abrams to charge that Mr. Kemp was trying "to tilt the playing field in his favor." Mr. Kemp claimed a voter registration group tied to Ms. Abrams had "submitted sloppy forms."

Since the 2010 election, twenty-four states overwhelmingly controlled by Republicans have put in place new voting restrictions, such as tougher voter ID laws, cutbacks to early voting, and barriers to registration. Republicans say these measures are necessary to combat the threat of widespread voter fraud, even though study after study shows that such fraud is exceedingly rare. Many of these states have hotly contested races in 2018, and a drop in turnout among Democratic constituencies, such as young people and voters of color, could keep Republicans in power.

This month, the Supreme Court upheld a law in North Dakota that could block seventy thousand residents who don't have a qualifying ID from the polls, including five thousand Native American voters. The law is particularly burdensome for Native Americans because it requires an ID with a "current residential street address," but some Native Americans live on reservations and get their mail through post office boxes. This is worrisome news for Senator Heidi Heitkamp, a Democrat, who is trailing her Republican opponent in the polls. She won election to the Senate in 2012 by three thousand votes, thanks largely to 80 percent support from the two counties with large Indian reservations.

In Florida, where Andrew Gillum, a Democrat, is running for governor—he would be the state's first black governor—1.6 million ex-felons won't be able to vote in this year's election, including almost half a million African Americans. Florida is one of only four states that prevent ex-felons from voting unless they're pardoned by the governor. The architect of the current law, Governor

Rick Scott, a Republican, is running for the Senate. Mr. Scott's predecessor, Governor Charlie Crist, a Republican who later switched parties, restored voting rights to 155,000 ex-felons; of those who registered to vote in 2012, 59 percent signed up as Democrats.

But Mr. Scott, who won two elections as governor by just sixty thousand votes, reversed that policy and has restored voting rights to just a little more than three thousand people while in office, with white ex-felons twice as likely to have their rights restored compared with African Americans. He's now locked in a dead heat with Senator Bill Nelson, a Democrat. Though there's an amendment on the ballot that would restore voting rights to up to 1.4 million ex-felons in the state, those directly impacted by Mr. Scott's felon disenfranchisement law won't be able to vote this year. Nearly one hundred thousand people who were on track to get their rights restored under Mr. Crist lost that chance when Mr. Scott changed the rules—a stark example of the precariousness of voting rights.

Voter suppression isn't just a potential problem in 2018—it seems to have already had a decisive impact in recent years. In 2016, the year of the first presidential election with Wisconsin's voter ID law in place, the state saw a plunge in black voter turnout, which undoubtedly helped Donald Trump carry the state. A study by the University of Wisconsin-Madison found that the ID requirement kept up to twenty-three thousand people from voting in two of the state's most Democratic counties, Milwaukee County and Madison's Dane County; African Americans were more than three times as likely as whites to be deterred from voting by the law. Mr. Trump won the state by twenty-three thousand votes. "It is very probable," Milwaukee's top election official, Neil Albrecht, told me last year, that "enough people were prevented from voting to have changed the outcome of the presidential election in Wisconsin." The ID requirement remains in effect today, and its biggest cheerleader, the Republican governor, Scott Walker, who claimed it was "a load of crap" that the law kept people from the polls, is locked in a close race for reelection against Tony Evers, a Democrat.

The most vociferous supporter of tightening access to the ballot, the Kansas secretary of state, Kris Kobach, former vice chairman of President Trump's election integrity commission, is also running for governor this year. A voter ID law Mr. Kobach championed led to a 2 percent decrease in turnout in 2012, according to a study by the Government Accountability Office, with the largest drop-off among young, black, and newly registered voters. Mr. Kobach won his primary in the governor's race by just 350 votes and is now in an extremely tight race against Laura Kelly, a Democrat, and an independent candidate, Greg Orman, so even a tiny reduction in participation among Democratic constituencies could put him in the governor's mansion. Since Mr. Kobach became secretary of state in 2011, more than twelve hundred ballots have been tossed because voters showed up at the polls without a sufficient ID, a much larger number than the fifteen cases of voter fraud his office has prosecuted.

Nowhere have hopes for high Democratic turnout collided with the reality of suppressive voting laws more than in Texas. In 2016, there were 3 million unregistered voters of color in the state, including 2.2 million unregistered Latinos and 750,000 unregistered African Americans. Though Texas set a new voter registration record this year, it's unlikely that the number of unregistered Latinos and African Americans has changed much. Texas has the most restrictive voter registration law in the country—to register voters, you must be deputized by a county and can register voters only in the county you're deputized in. The number of unregistered voters of color is a major obstacle for the Democratic candidate Beto

O'Rourke in his race against Senator Ted Cruz. Though the demographics of the state suggest that it should be trending purple, the state's voting rules help keep it red.

Chief Justice John Roberts, in the 2013 Supreme Court ruling he wrote that gutted the Voting Rights Act, dismissed the idea that voting discrimination was still "flagrant" and "widespread." Instead he wrote, "Our country has changed." Yet since that decision, state and local governments that formerly had to approve their voting changes with the federal government, like Georgia and Texas, have closed 20 percent more polling places per capita than other states have, many in neighborhoods with large minority populations. More than half the states freed from federal oversight have put in place new voting restrictions in recent years. The 2016 election had the unfortunate distinction of being the first presidential contest in fifty years without the full protections of the Voting Rights Act; in 2018, the threat of disenfranchisement has gotten worse, in the South and beyond.

People tend to focus on obstacles to voting when they believe it will affect a close election, as in Georgia. But efforts to erect barriers to the ballot box are wrong regardless of whether they decide the outcome of an election. If Democrats turn out in large numbers on November 6, as the early-voting data suggests is happening in some key states, it will be in spite of these barriers, not because they didn't exist or didn't matter.

Despite rampant suppression efforts, there is some hope. In seven states, ballot initiatives would restore voting rights to ex-felons, make it easier to register to vote, and crack down on gerrymandering. If these pass, we could see 2018 as a turning point for expanding voting rights, instead of an election tainted by voter suppression. But first people need to have the right to cast a ballot.

Stacey Abrams, Brian Kemp, and Neo–Jim Crow in Georgia

CAROL ANDERSON

New York Times, November 7, 2018

So much has been written about the election for governor in Georgia between the Democrat Stacey Abrams, who would be the first black woman in that role, and Brian Kemp, her Republican opponent, a race that may not be over as they wait for absentee and provisional ballots to be counted.

But it was bracing to see the election through the eyes of black people who had to deal with Jim Crow, who remembered the euphoria of Barack Obama's wins, who witnessed the hatred and obstruction he endured for eight years, and who now have to grapple with the rising swamp of neo–Jim Crow. Mr. Kemp, the man who controls the elections in the state while also vying for governor, has done everything in his power to block African Americans from casting their ballots.

All of that was clear on election day, as I drove people who needed a ride to their polling stations. One of my passengers was ninety and had voted in every election since she was eighteen. As we pulled away from the polls, she latched onto a memory.

In Georgia, she recalled, officials at a polling station made her read something before she was allowed to vote. "Read something," she kept repeating. She was talking about the literacy test, which had reduced black voter registration in some areas in the South to less than 10 percent and which only the legal power of the Voting Rights Act of 1965 had stopped.

But since 2013, when the Supreme Court gutted section 4 of the act, that power to prevent the use of discriminatory devices has been greatly hobbled. That was evident as my nonagenarian passenger struggled to pull out of her wallet a government-issued photo ID so that the poll workers, who have known her for decades, could allow her to vote.

In addition to voter ID laws, Georgia had implemented a program called "exact match" that a judge had previously ruled was racially discriminatory but was, nonetheless, reborn with all of its defects by the Georgia legislature and in full operation in 2018. This voter registration program was its own literacy test as it required information on the voter registration card to be an exact image of that stored in a state database or Social Security office. An accent or hyphen in one better be there in the other. In this election alone, Mr. Kemp had trapped fifty-three thousand voter registration cards using exact match, and 70 percent of the applicants kicked into electoral purgatory were African American, including one of my colleagues, a faculty member at Emory University.

Then there was the basic election processes that wreaked havoc at the polls. Voting machines in Snellville in metro Atlanta arrived with no power cords. People were waiting for hours in a line that was not moving and were finally forced to leave without voting because they had to get to their jobs. This was the same area where absentee ballots were rejected at almost ten times the state average.

Those neo–Jim Crow barriers were rising up from Georgia's Confederate soil like ghosts.

And I kept driving. Another one of my passengers was well into her eighties. She had a special type of wisdom. Sometimes it came like ice and other times like fire. She looked at me while we were coming back from the polls and remarked that she was proud to be able to vote for Ms. Abrams.

Then came the burn. "Stacey Abrams is smart," she said with a smile. "Just like Obama. Smart. And," as the smile melted away, "they will hate her just as much."

That line stung. It embodied the bittersweet mixture of pride in black achievement and sorrow for the pain that would come, because the things this nation claims are attributes, like intelligence, actually make African Americans targets.

She remembered how it allowed someone like the woefully inarticulate Donald Trump to believe he had the right to demand President Obama's birth certificate and also transcripts from Columbia and Harvard.

It meant that a Republican-dominated Congress could shower down disrespect on President Obama—from Representative Joe Wilson's "You lie!" to Senator Mitch McConnell's unprecedented refusal to even hold hearings for the president's nominee to the Supreme Court, Merrick Garland. It meant twisting Mr. Obama's signature and lifesaving legislative achievement, the Affordable Care Act, into a monstrosity of socialized "death panels."

What that kind of hatred meant for Stacey Abrams, who just might face a highly gerrymandered state legislature, was chilling. We were silent the rest of the car ride.

As I returned home, the election results appeared to answer that question. But only for now.

We Cannot Resign Ourselves to Dismay and Disenfranchisement

STACEY ABRAMS

New York Times, May 15, 2019

In the mid-1960s, when my father was a teenager, he was arrested. His crime? Registering black voters in Mississippi. He and my mother had joined the civil rights movement well before they were even old enough to vote themselves.

They braved this dangerous work, which all too often created martyrs of marchers. In doing so, my parents ingrained in their six children a deep and permanent reverence for the franchise. We were taught that the right to vote undergirds all other rights, that free and fair elections are necessary for social progress.

That is why I am determined to end voter suppression and empower all people to participate in our democracy.

True voter access means that every person has the right to register, cast a ballot, and have that ballot counted—without undue hardship. Unfortunately, the forces my parents battled fifty years ago continue to stifle democracy.

My home state, Georgia, for example, suffered a vicious blend of electoral malfeasance, misfeasance, and mismanagement during my race for governor last fall. But Georgia is not alone.

Local and state officials across the country, emboldened by the Supreme Court effectively neutering the Voting Rights Act in *Shelby County v. Holder* in 2013, are shamelessly weakening voter registration, ballot access, and ballot-counting procedures.

These officials slyly mask their assaults through criteria that appear neutral on the surface but nevertheless target race, gender, language, and economic status. The "exact match" policy in Georgia, which a federal court deemed unlawful in November because it requires perfect data entry to secure a timely registration, serves as one example of such a policy.

Although "exact match" lacks the explicit racial animus of Jim Crow, its execution nonetheless betrayed its true purpose to disenfranchise voters of color. Georgia's secretary of state held fifty-three thousand voter registrations hostage under exact match last year, 70 percent of which came from black voters, who made up only around 30 percent of Georgia's eligible voters.

The state officials behind exact match were well aware, per an earlier lawsuit, that when only a missing hyphen or a typo in a government database can form the basis to withhold the right to vote, people of color will bear the brunt of such trivial mistakes.

A particularly egregious example involved a voter whose last name is "del Rio." He was affected by the policy merely because the Department of Motor Vehicles office where he registered to vote did not allow spaces in last names. He was "delRio" there. But the voter rolls do allow spaces. No exact match. Voters like Mr. del Rio faced unnecessary hurdles, and poll workers were not trained properly to make sure that voices like his were heard.

Across the country, voter purges employ an easily manipulated "use it or lose it" rule, under which eligible voters who exercised their First Amendment right to abstain from voting in prior elections can be booted off the rolls.

Add to this mix closed or relocated polling places outside the reach of public transit, sometimes as far as seventy-five miles away, or long lines that force low-income voters to forfeit half a day's pay, and a modern poll tax is revealed.

State legislatures have continued the trend this year. In Texas, officials are attempting to further criminalize eligible voters for inadvertent errors often caused by language barriers. In Tennessee, a state with notoriously low voter turnout, the legislature approved a bill subjecting third-party groups conducting voter registration drives to onerous requirements under threat of civil and criminal penalty.

In Florida, 1.4 million Floridians with felonies were reenfranchised with a constitutional amendment last year that passed with 65 percent of the vote—the largest expansion of voting rights in a half century. But the legislature has contravened the will of the people, once again disenfranchising hundreds of thousands of returning citizens through a bill that imposes an antiquated poll tax on them in the form of court fees.

After voters run gantlets to get on the rolls, they are undermined by the mismanagement of inexact voter databases, ancient and underresourced machines, lost absentee ballots, or by elections officials who refuse to count votes that were properly cast.

On election night 2018, as phones rang with tales of missing machines, provisional ballots allocated by a vague lottery system, and regular voters vanishing from the rolls, I made a simple demand: Count every vote.

Over the next ten days, my campaign logged over forty thousand calls of voter suppression, sent out volunteers to help voters make sure their provisional ballots were counted, and quickly filed numerous lawsuits. Amid this chaos, the results of the election were certified. We demonstrated the immensity of the problem, yet opponents to voting rights responded with the specious claim that increased turnout was somehow proof that no suppression had occurred.

That argument is shameful. A record number of black, Latino, and Asian American / Pacific Islander voters turned out in Georgia to support an inclusive agenda, which led to even more of those voters being subjected to voter suppression.

Voters of color endured three-, four-, and five-hour lines on election day precisely because so many who turned out to vote were confronted with underresourced precincts and faulty voting machines. Unprecedented turnout led to countless thousands being blocked or turned away.

The state's top elections official, former secretary of state Brian Kemp himself—functioning simultaneously as the scorekeeper, referee, and contestant in the gubernatorial election—was caught revealing to supporters that he was "concerned" about record absentee ballot requests from voters of color.

In response, I redoubled my commitment to voting rights and started a nonprofit called Fair Fight Action to harness the commitment and urgency of Georgians who reported, by a 52 percent margin, that they believe suppression affected 2018 election outcomes.

This distrust, shared by millions of others nationwide, should alarm every American; democracy should not differ so dramatically across state and, worse, county lines, where hyperlocal suppressive tactics like the proposed closing of most polling places in a majority-black South Georgia county last year can slip under the radar.

That's why we filed a federal voting rights case three weeks after election day, demanding that Georgia's elections system comply with constitutional obligations and requirements under federal law, including those provisions of the Voting Rights Act that remain in force, and we asked that Georgia be required to preclear voting changes again with the Justice Department before taking effect.

We ask for proper and uniform training of poll workers, timely processing of absentee ballots, functioning and secure voting machines, accurate voter registration databases, an end to policies like "exact match" and "use it or lose it," and many more necessary remedies.

Facing an existential crisis of democracy, Americans cannot resign ourselves to disenfranchisement and dismay. We must find hope in the energy of voters who supported access to healthcare, economic opportunity, and high-quality public education in record numbers.

This is our ethos: Use the ballot box to create the change our communities need and deserve. In Georgia and across our country, voters deserve the right to pick their leaders and set the direction of our nation. And we shall not rest until this democracy is fully realized.

Statement of Stacey Y. Abrams, Founder & Chair, Fair Fight Action on Continuing Challenges to the Voting Rights Act since *Shelby County v. Holder* before the House Judiciary's Subcommittee on the Constitution, Civil Rights, and Civil Liberties, June 25, 2019

STACEY ABRAMS

Chairman Cohen, Ranking Member Johnson, Committee Members, thank you for allowing me to address this important hearing today, marking six years since the U.S. Supreme Court issued its decision in *Shelby County v. Holder*, a decision that has dramatically undermined access to full participation in our democracy by effectively negating the core mechanism for preventing voter suppression as enshrined in the 1965 Voting Rights Act. In so doing, the *Shelby* decision created a new channel for the troubling practice of voter suppression, during a time of dramatic demographic change, and thus has permitted the proliferation of laws and practices that seek to stymie a fundamental exercise of citizenship. However, no assault on democracy will ever be limited to its targets. As the franchise is weakened, all citizens feel the effects and even the perpetrators eventually face the consequences of collateral damage—an erosion of our democracy writ large.

I come today because I was raised in Mississippi, where my parents joined the civil rights movement as teenagers and where, in the wake of the Voting Rights Act, they cherished their right to vote and instilled in their six children a deep reverence for the franchise. I came of age in Georgia, where I registered voters in college, served as House Democratic Leader and founder of a voting rights organization, and where I stood for office as the Democratic nominee for governor in 2018, an election plagued by voter-suppression tactics all too common in a post-*Shelby* world.

Jurisdictions formerly covered under section 5 have raced to reinstate or create new hurdles to voter registration, access to the ballot box, and ballot counting. New states facing changes to their voter composition have likewise taken up this opposition to full citizen participation by implementing rules that, while facially neutral, result in a disturbingly predictable effect on voter access among minority citizens. Among the states, however, Georgia has been one of the most aggressive in leveraging the lack of federal oversight to use both law and policy to actualize voter-suppression efforts that target voters of color.

I. VOTER REGISTRATION IMPEDIMENTS

As founder of the New Georgia Project, one of the state's largest voter registration organizations, I learned firsthand how insidious Georgia's post-*Shelby* obstacles to voter registration have become. Our organization conducted voter registration across 159 counties, well aware that for low-propensity voters, this type of in-person registration is most effective. Third-party voter registration is a critical path to engaging citizens of colors in the democratic process, and minorities are twice as likely to register through a voter registration drive than are whites.

In its report, *State Restrictions on Voter Registration Drives*, which focuses on the challenges posed across the country, the Brennan Center highlights research about the importance of third-party voter registration for racial and ethnic minorities—namely nearly double the likelihood of registration from these efforts.[1] Specifically, "[i]n 2004, while 7.4% of non-Hispanic whites registered with private voter registration drives, 12.7% of Blacks and 12.9% of Hispanics did the same. In 2008, African Americans and Hispanics nationally remained almost twice as likely to register through a voter registration drive as whites. While 5% of non-Hispanic whites registered at private voter registration drives, 11.1% of African Americans and 9.6% of Hispanics did the same. [In] the 2010 election, 4.4% of non-Hispanic whites registered at private drives, as compared to 7.2% of African-Americans and 8.9% of Hispanics."

These registration efforts not only create new registrants but also serve to create new and active voters. Research completed by Dr. David Nickerson at the University of Notre Dame sought to understand the impact of drives on voting.[2] To this end, the researchers conducted experiments run in Detroit and Kalamazoo, Michigan, and Tampa, Florida, the results of which demonstrate that 20 percent of low-income citizens who register in a door-to-door drive actually go out and vote. Their findings control for type of election year (municipal, presidential, midterm) as well as turnout activities and serve as a baseline to understand what we can expect from a voter registration drive focusing on underrepresented groups.

1   http://www.brennancenter.org/sites/default/files/legacy/publications/State%20Restrictions%20on%20Voter%20Registration%20Drives.pdf
2   https://www3.nd.edu/~dnickers/files/papers/Nickerson_Registration_temp.pdf

There is no doubt a direct correlation between the effectiveness of such efforts, and the post-*Shelby* legislation, and efforts in states like Georgia, Tennessee, North Carolina, Texas, and Florida to impede these activities.

a. Lack of Transparency—Blackout Periods and Exact Match

Through our project and in cooperation with other organizations that work to increase registration among communities of color, we tracked the processing of forms, and we proactively attempted to collaborate with the office of the secretary of state. In response to our efforts, which submitted thousands of verified forms, then-Georgia secretary of state Brian Kemp, and those he oversaw as the state's election superintendent, refused to process registration forms in a timely manner.

As a result, we uncovered unpublished internal rules such as the ninety-day blackout period during which no voter registration forms were processed and which resulted in untimely delays. Only due to a federal lawsuit in 2017 during a special congressional election were citizens able to effectively challenge and eliminate this secret policy. Under a fully functional Voting Rights Act, no such period would be permitted without preclearance and transparency.

Due to the unprecedented number of applications submitted from primarily voters of color, we also uncovered the racially discriminatory effect of the "exact match process" that disproportionately captures voters of color. Exact match requires perfect data entry by state employees to secure a proper registration in Georgia. In 2009, under preclearance requirements, the Justice Department summarily rejected exact match as presenting "real," "substantial," and "retrogressive" burdens on voters of color.[3]

Post-*Shelby*, the policy took effect and led to more than thirty-four thousand applications being suspended under the system, including thousands submitted in 2014. Once the use of exact match was uncovered, in 2016, a group of organizations filed suit in federal court. Mr. Kemp agreed to a settlement and processing of those delayed applications. However, in the following state legislative session, another iteration of exact match passed through the Georgia legislature despite his 2016 federal court settlement. This use of exact match led to fifty-three thousand voter registrations being held hostage in 2018, 80 percent of whom were people of color and 70 percent of whom were black voters, who comprise roughly 30 percent of Georgia's eligible voters. In 2018, Georgia officials lost another lawsuit pertaining to exact match.

In the period between 2015 and 2018, federal courts admonished both blackout periods and multiple iterations of the exact match process; however, absent a robust preclearance process, these remedies came too late for participants in the 2014, 2016, and 2018 state and federal elections, as well as other elections where voters had no notice of these processes.

b. Excessive Voter Purges

The right to vote begins with being able to get on the rolls, but remaining on the voter rolls has also been implicated by the gutting of the Voting Rights Act. Post-*Shelby*, the former secretary of state misappropriated practical devices approved to maintain

3   https://www.justice.gov/crt/voting-determination-letter-58

accurate voter files and instead undermined lawful access to the franchise. Under his regime and without the oversight of the Justice Department, facially neutral rules for removing voters who have died or left the state, as demonstrated by tracking voter behavior, have instead become tools for voter purges, where longtime voters find themselves cast from the rolls, forced to prove their rights against an indifferent bureaucracy.

During his tenure, in a state with six million voters, the former secretary of state removed over 1.4 million voters from the rolls. In July 2017, four years free from preclearance scrutiny, he removed more than half a million voters from the rolls in a single day, reducing the number of registered voters in Georgia by 8 percent.[4] An estimated 107,000 of these voters were removed through a "use-it-or-lose-it" scheme, under which eligible Georgia voters were designated for removal merely for not having voted in prior elections, something that is a First Amendment right.[5] The process for removal is also shrouded in inefficiencies and challenges, as a number of those removed could demonstrate regular voting patterns.

Of 159 counties in Georgia, 156 counties removed a higher rate of voters from the rolls post-*Shelby*, which resulted in an increase in the number of voters being forced to cast provisional ballots.[6] While the availability of provisional ballots may be seen as a remedy, the operative concern is why the vast majority of counties, with the tacit approval of the secretary of state, forces citizens to traverse a gauntlet of additional obstacles to exercise a fundamental right.

4   https://www.apmreports.org/story/2018/10/19/georgia-voter-purge
5   Ibid.
6   https://www.brennancenter.org/sites/default/files/publications/Purges
    _Growing_Threat_2018.pdf

II. OBSTACLES TO BALLOT ACCESS AND
BALLOT COUNTING

As vital as preclearance had been to access to registration, the most pernicious effect of its absence can be found in the very act of casting a vote. Section 5 provided an effective check against hyperlocal suppressive tactics that often fly under the radar, like the proposed closing of seven of nine polling places in a majority-black South Georgia county last year, or the erroneous institution of "challenge" proceedings against voters of color, including troubling cases in 2015.[7] These groups are forced to scramble considerable resources and organize from a defensive posture. Even in ostensibly positive actions, like in-person early voting, some jurisdictions have opted to locate the sole venue in the police department / judicial complex, where poor relations with law enforcement serve as a chilling effect on engagement. Section 5's restoration would require a clear-eyed and thoughtful calculus not currently mandated.

Last election cycle, Georgia officials lost a series of lawsuits pertaining to access to the ballot and the counting of votes. Over several days, separate federal courts ruled against policies for rejecting absentee ballots and ballot applications under trivial pretenses, for implementing a haphazard and inconsistent provisional balloting system, and for improperly disallowing access to translators in the polling booth. However, these practices have proliferated since the suspension of section 5, and while these lawsuits brought remedy to some, thousands more may have faced similar discrimination without the resources or the knowledge to gain relief.

The core value of the Voting Rights Act was to, at last, create equal access to the ballot, irrespective of race, class, or partisanship.

---

7   https://www.usccr.gov/pubs/2018/Minority_Voting_Access_2018.pdf at 139.

Yet, by denying the real and present danger posed by those who see voters of color as a threat to be neutralized rather than as fellow citizens to be engaged, *Shelby* has destabilized the whole of our democratic experiment. Rather than a Justice Department that prevents discriminatory voting policies from taking effect in the first place, the Supreme Court created a system of disproportionate impact, one in which justice could prevail in select instances and only after multiple federal courts intervened.

As a result, post-*Shelby*, groups dedicated to expanding the franchise for voters of color instead must traverse an obstacle course of discriminatory voting practices, through resource-intensive litigation and advocacy work often aimed at yet another permutation of the same discriminatory policies like exact match, targeted poll closures, or rejected absentee ballots. This antivoting system has the concomitant effect of harming taxpayers, as voter suppressors nonchalantly expend tax dollars to defend voter suppression in court.

At the end of the 2018 contest, I acknowledged the legal result of an election marred by widespread election irregularities. The rules of the process permitted some dubious actions, ignored unconstitutional behaviors, and encouraged an abdication of responsibility by too many charged with the guardianship of this sacred trust. Therefore, I have redoubled my commitment to voting rights through the creation of Fair Fight Action. Fair Fight has filed a federal lawsuit against the Georgia secretary of state, asking for Georgia's preclearance requirement to be reinstated under section 3 of the Voting Rights Act. Our groundbreaking lawsuit involves numerous coplaintiffs including Ebenezer Baptist Church, the ancestral congregation of the Reverend Dr. Martin Luther King Jr.

We are hopeful for judicial relief from voter suppression, including the prevention of any future racially discriminatory voting changes. Costly litigation bankrolled by taxpayers should not be necessary, and members of Congress from both parties should fulfill their responsibility to protect voters of color in Georgia and across the country.

The currently proposed Voting Rights Advancement Act and Voting Rights Amendment Act represent considerable promise toward restoring the preclearance protections of the original Voting Rights Act, including needed modern-day protections like requiring nationwide preclearance to prohibit known discriminatory practices.[8] I urge Congress to act on them as top priorities.

Thank you again for this opportunity to appear today.

8   https://sewell.house.gov/media-center/press-releases/sewell-leahy
    -introduce-voting-rights-advancement-act

Bibliography

BOOKS

Abrams, Stacey. *Lead from the Outside: How to Build Your Future and Make Real Change*. New York: Picador, 2019.

Anderson, Carol. *One Person, No Vote: How Voter Suppression Is Destroying Our Democracy*. New York: Bloomsbury, 2018.

———. *White Rage: The Unspoken Truth of Our Racial Divide*. New York: Bloomsbury, 2016.

Anderson, Eric. *Race and Politics in North Carolina, 1872–1901: The Black Second*. Baton Rouge: Louisiana State University Press, 1980.

Behrend, Justin. *Reconstructing Democracy: Grassroots Black Politics in the Deep South after the Civil War*. Athens: University of Georgia Press, 2015.

Berman, Ari. *Give Us the Ballot: The Modern Struggle for Voting Rights in America*. New York: Farrar, Straus and Giroux, 2015.

Blain, Keisha N. *Set the World on Fire: Black Nationalist Women and the Global Struggle for Freedom*. Philadelphia: University of Pennsylvania Press, 2018.

Brown-Nagin, Tomiko. *Courage to Dissent: Atlanta and the Long History of the Civil Rights Movement*. New York: Oxford University Press, 2011.

Chafe, William Henry. *Civilities and Civil Rights: Greensboro, North Carolina, and the Black Struggle for Freedom*. Oxford: Oxford University Press, 1992.

Crespino, Joseph. *In Search of Another Country: Mississippi and the Conservative Counterrevolution*. Princeton, N.J.: Princeton University Press, 2009.

Dittmer, John. *Local People: The Struggle for Civil Rights in Mississippi*. Champaign: University of Illinois Press, 1994.

Downs, Jim. *Sick from Freedom: African American Illness and Suffering during the Civil War and Reconstruction*. New York: Oxford University Press, 2012.

Faulkenbury, Evan. *Poll Power: The Voter Education Project and the Movement for the Ballot in the American South*. Chapel Hill: University of North Carolina Press, 2019.

Foner, Eric. *Reconstruction: America's Unfinished Business, 1863–1877*. New York: Harper and Row, 1988.

———. *The Second Founding: How the Civil War and Reconstruction Remade the Constitution*. New York: Norton, 2019.

Frystak, Shannon. *Our Minds on Freedom: Women and the Struggle for Black Equality in Louisiana, 1924–1967*. Baton Rouge: Louisiana State University Press, 2009.

Gilmore, Glenda Elizabeth. *Defying Dixie: The Radical Roots of Civil Rights, 1919–1950*. New York: Norton, 2008.

———. *Gender and Jim Crow: Women and the Politics of White Supremacy in North Carolina, 1896–1920*. Chapel Hill: University of North Carolina Press, 1996.

Hahn, Steven. *A Nation under Our Feet: Black Political Struggles in the Rural South from Slavery to the Great Migration*. Cambridge: Harvard University Press, 2005.

Jones, Martha S. *Birthright Citizens: A History of Race and Rights in Antebellum America*. New York: Cambridge University Press, 2018.

Keyssar, Alexander. *The Right to Vote: The Contested History of Democracy in the United States*. New York: Basic Books, 2000.

Kousser, J. Morgan. *The Shaping of Southern Politics: Suffrage Restriction and the Establishment of the One-Party South*. New Haven: Yale University Press, 1974.

Kruse, Kevin. *White Flight: Atlanta and the Making of Modern Conservatism*. Princeton, N.J.: Princeton University Press, 2005.

Lassiter, Matthew D. *The Silent Majority: Suburban Politics in the Sunbelt South*. Princeton, N.J.: Princeton University Press, 2006.

McDonald, Laughlin. *American Indians and the Fight for Equal Voting Rights*. Norman. University of Oklahoma Press, 2010.

Perman, Michael. *Struggle for Mastery: Disfranchisement in the South*. Chapel Hill: University of North Carolina Press, 2001.

Ransby, Barbara. *Ella Baker and the Black Freedom Movement: A Radical Democratic Vision*. Chapel Hill: University of North Carolina Press, 2003.

Richardson, Heather Cox. *The Death of Reconstruction: Race, Labor, and Politics in the Post–Civil War North, 1865–1901*. Cambridge: Harvard University Press, 2001.

———. *To Make Men Free: A History of the Republican Party*. New York: Basic, 2014.

Riser, R. Volney. *Defying Disfranchisement: Black Voting Rights Activism in the Jim Crow South*. Baton Rouge: LSU Press, 2010.

Rosen, Hannah. *Terror in the Heart of Freedom: Citizenship, Sexual Violence, and the Meaning of Race in the Postemancipation South*. Chapel Hill: University of North Carolina Press, 2009.

Sokol, Jason. *There Goes My Everything: White Southerners in the Age of Civil Rights, 1945–1975*. New York: Knopf, 2006.

Sturkey, William. *Hattiesburg: An American City in Black and White*. Cambridge, Mass.: Harvard University Press, 2019.

Terborg-Penn, Rosalyn. *African American Women in the Struggle for the Vote, 1850–1929*. Bloomington: Indiana University Press, 1988.

Woodward, C. Vann. *Origins of the New South, 1877–1913*. Baton Rouge: Louisiana State University Press, 1951.

———. *The Strange Career of Jim Crow*. New York: Oxford University Press, 1955.

ARTICLES

Adams, J. Christian. "In *Shelby County v. Holder*, Supreme Court Will Decide Integrity of Future Elections." *Forbes*, June 13, 2013. https://www.forbes.com/sites/realspin/2013/06/13/in-shelby-county-v

-holder-supreme-court-will-decide-integrity-of-future-elections
/#4451a05b77af.

Anderson, Carol. "Opinion: The Republican Approach to Voter Fraud:
Lie." *New York Times*, September 8, 2018. https://www.nytimes
.com/2018/09/08/opinion/sunday/voter-fraud-lie-missouri.html.

———. "Opinion: Stacey Abrams, Brian Kemp, and Neo–Jim Crow in
Georgia." *New York Times*, November 7, 2018. https://www.nytimes
.com/2018/11/07/opinion/stacey-abrams-election-governor-georgia
.html.

———. "Opinion: Voting While Black: The Racial Injustice that Harms
Our Democracy." *The Guardian*, June 7, 2018. https://www
.theguardian.com/commentisfree/2018/jun/07/black-voter
-suppression-rights-america-trump.

Badger, Emily. "What if Everyone Voted?" *New York Times*, October 29,
2018. https://www.nytimes.com/2018/10/29/upshot/what-if
-everyone-voted.html.

Barber, William, II. "Op-Ed: Wake Up! Voter Suppression Is Not Dead."
Essence, October 18, 2018. https://www.essence.com/news/politics
/voter-suppression-is-not-dead/.

Bazelon, Emily. "Voting Rights 2.0." *Slate*, February 11, 2013. http://
www.slate.com/articles/news_and_politics/jurisprudence/2013/02
/the_voting_rights_act_and_shelby_county_v_holder_how_the
_supreme_court_could.html.

———. "Will Florida's Ex-felons Finally Regain the Right to Vote?"
New York Times Magazine, September 26, 2108. https://www.nytimes
.com/2018/09/26/magazine/ex-felons-voting-rights-florida.html.

Berman, Ari. "Commentary: 5 Myths about Gerrymandering." *Chicago
Tribune*, March 8, 2018. https://www.chicagotribune.com/news
/opinion/commentary/ct-perspec-gerrymandering-maps-elections
-politics-myths-0309-20180308-story.html. Washington Post, same
date, https://www.washingtonpost.com/outlook/five-myths/five
-myths-about-gerrymandering/2018/03/08/f9d1a230-2241-11e8-badd
-7c9f29a55815_story.html?utm_term=.5ffcf8deb367.

Berman, Ari. "Opinion: How Voter Suppression Could Swing the Midterms." *New York Times*, October 27, 2018. https://www.nytimes .com/2018/10/27/opinion/sunday/voter-suppression-georgia-2018 .html.

Berman, Ari. "Why the Voting Rights Act Is Once Again under Threat." *New York Times,* August 6, 2015. https://www.nytimes.com/2015/08 /06/opinion/why-the-voting-rights-act-is-once-again-under-threat .html.

Blight, David W. "Voter Suppression, Then and Now." *New York Times*, September 7, 2012. https://www.nytimes.com/2012/09/07/opinion /frederick-douglass-and-voter-fraud.html.

Brotheron, David. "Opinion: A Front-Row Seat to Voter Suppression in Georgia." *Seattle Times*, November 8, 2018. https://www.seattletimes .com/opinion/a-front-row-seat-to-voter-suppression-in-georgia/.

Burmila, Edward. "How to Fight Voter Suppression in 2018." *Dissent*, July 11, 2018. https://www.dissentmagazine.org/online_articles /how-to-fight-voter-suppression-tactics-2018-practical-guide.

Burton, Vernon. "Race and Reconstruction: Edgefield County, South Carolina." *Journal of Social History* 12, no. 1 (Fall, 1978): 31.

Cobb, Jelani. "Voter-Suppression Tactics in the Age of Trump." *New Yorker*, October 29, 2018. https://www.newyorker.com/magazine /2018/10/29/voter-suppression-tactics-in-the-age-of-trump.

Downs, Gregory. "Today's Voter Suppression Tactics Have a 150 Year History." *Talking Points Memo*, July 26, 2018. https:// talkingpointsmemo.com/feature/todays-voter-suppression -tactics-have-a-150-year-history.

Greenhouse, Linda. "Opinion: Two Ways of Looking at Gerrymandering." *New York Times*, January 4, 2018. https://www .nytimes.com/2018/01/04/opinion/gerrymandering-supreme-court .html.

Hall, Jacqueline Dowd. "The Long Civil Rights Movement and the Political Uses of the Past." *Journal of American History* 91, no. 4 (2005).

Hasen, Richard L. "Is the Assault on Voting Rights Getting Worse, or Are We Just Noticing It More?" *Slate*, October 23, 2018. https://slate .com/news-and-politics/2018/10/brian-kemp-kris-kobach-voter -suppression.html?wpsrc=sh_all_dt_tw_ru.

Ho, Dale. "Opinion: The Ohio Purge and the Future of Voting." *New York Times*, June 12, 2018. https://www.nytimes.com/2018/06/12 /opinion/the-ohio-purge-and-the-future-of-voting.html.

Holder, Eric, Jr. "Commentary: Gerrymandering Has Broken Our Democracy. The Supreme Court Should Help Fix It." *Chicago Tribune*, October 3, 2017. https://www.chicagotribune.com/news /opinion/commentary/ct-gerrymandering-supreme-court-wisconsin -20171003-story.html.

Hunter, Marcus Anthony. "Opinion: Voter Suppression Is a Threat to All." *Washington Post*, January 20, 2014. https://www.washingtonpost .com/opinions/voter-suppression-is-a-threat-to-all/2014/01/19 /abc56154-7fa6-11e3-9556-4a4bf7bcbd84_story. html?utm_term=.083d4d3f86f1.

Johnson, Earl C. "Op-Ed: Voter ID on the N.C. Ballot Is about Suppression, Not Fraud." *News & Observer*, July 11, 2018. https://www .newsobserver.com/opinion/op-ed/article214681510.html.

Keyssar, Alexander. "The Strange Career of Voter Suppression." *New York Times, Campaign Stops* blog, February 12, 2012. https://campaignstops .blogs.nytimes.com/2012/02/12/the-strange-career-of-voter -suppression/.

———. "Who Gets to Vote?" *New York Times*, September 30, 2016. https://www.nytimes.com/2016/10/02/opinion/sunday/who-gets -to-vote.html.

Knight, Frederick. "Georgia Election Fight Shows Black Voter Suppression, a Southern Traditions, Still Flourishes." *PBS News Hour*, October 28, 2018. https://www.pbs.org/newshour/politics/georgia -election-fight-shows-that-black-voter-suppression-a-southern -tradition-still-flourishes.

———. "Voter ID Laws Why Democrats Fight for the Ballot in Mississippi Still Matters." *The Conversation*, August 22, 2016. http://theconversation.com/voter-id-laws-why-black-democrats-fight-for-the-ballot-in-mississippi-still-matters-63583.

Lawrence, Regina. "Guest Column: Civic Engagement and the Future of Texas." *Texas Tribune*, June 4, 2013. https://www.texastribune.org/2013/06/04/guest-column-civic-engagement-and-future-texas/.

Lawson, Steven, and Darryl Paulson. "Opinion Column: A Renewed Attack on Voting Rights." *Tampa Bay Times*, March 29, 2019. https://www.tampabay.com/opinion/columns/column-a-renewed-attack-on-voting-rights-20190329/.

Lewis, John. "Why We Still Need the Voting Rights Act." *Washington Post*, February 24, 2013. https://www.washingtonpost.com/opinions/why-we-still-need-the-voting-rights-act/2013/02/24/a70a930c-7d43-11e2-9a75-dab0201670da_story.html?utm_term=.12a931188190.

Lichtman, Allan. "Framers Fail: Voting Is a Basic Right but They Didn't Guarantee It in the Constitution." *USA Today*, September 26, 2018. https://www.usatoday.com/story/opinion/2018/09/26/republicans-owe-founders-voting-restrictions-no-guaranteed-right-column/1405645002/.

———. "Voter Fraud Isn't a Problem in America. Low Turnout Is." *Washington Post*, October 22, 2018. https://www.washingtonpost.com/outlook/2018/10/22/voter-fraud-isnt-problem-america-low-turnout-is/?utm_term=.e04d9d2dc331.

Little, Becky. "Native Americans Weren't Guaranteed the Right to Vote in Every State until 1962." *History.com*, November 6, 2018.

Mask, Deirdre. "Opinion: Where the Streets Have No Names, the People Have No Vote." *New York Times*, October 19, 2019. https://www.nytimes.com/2018/10/19/opinion/sunday/north-dakota-addresses-voting-id.html.

Merritt, Keri Leigh. "The Myth of a Southern Democracy." *Bitter Southerner*, November 1, 2018 [date inferred from piece]. https://

bittersoutherner.com/from-the-southern-perspective/the-myth-of
-southern-democracy-keri-leigh-merritt.

Mudde, Cas. "Opinion: Voter Suppression Is an All-American Problem
We Can Fight—and Win." *The Guardian*, November 16, 201. https://
www.theguardian.com/commentisfree/2018/nov/16/
us-midterm-elections-voter-suppression-fight-democrats-georgia.

Perry, Imani. "Voter Suppression Carries Slavery's Three-Fifths Clause
into the Present." *The Guardian*, January 31, 2019. https://www
.theguardian.com/commentisfree/2019/jan/31/voter-suppression
-african-american-james-madison-slavery.

Peters, Jeremy W. "Waiting Times at Ballot Boxes Draw Scrutiny." *New
York Times*, February 4, 2013. https://www.nytimes.com
/roomfordebate/2015/08/05/
ensuring-voting-rights-in-the-21st-century.

Railton, Ben. "Considering History: The Fight for Native American
Citizenship and Voting Rights." *Saturday Evening Post*, October 24,
2018. https://www.saturdayeveningpost.com/2018/10/considering
-history-the-fight-for-native-american-citizenship-and-voting-rights/.

Rothschild, Matt. "Op-Ed: The Fight against Voter Suppression." *Urban
Milwaukee*, October 17, 2018. https://urbanmilwaukee.com/2018/10
/17/op-ed-the-fight-against-voter-suppression/.

Schuessler, Jennifer. "The History behind the Birthright Citizenship
Ban." *New York Times*, July 19, 2018. https://www.nytimes.com/2018
/07/19/arts/the-history-behind-the-birthright-citizenship-battle
.html.

Shattuck, John. "The War on Voting Rights." *Boston Globe*, October 25,
2018. https://www.bostonglobe.com/opinion/2018/10/25/the-war
-voting-rights/fRNgPXEHiWhWOgk24Jo2cO/story.html.

Stebenne, David. "Re-mapping American Politics: The Redistricting
Revolution Fifty Years Later." *Origins*, February 2012. http://origins
.osu.edu/article/re-mapping-american-politics-redistricting
-revolution-fifty-years-later.

Stewart, Emily. "The Battle over Early Voting, Explained." *Vox*,
    November 4, 2018. https://www.vox.com/2018/10/29/18018634
    /early-voting-2018.

Swartz, Mimi. "The Voter Suppression State." *New York Times*, January
    31, 2019. https://www.nytimes.com/2019/01/31/opinion/texas-voter
    -suppression.html.

Thompson, Heather Ann. "Why Mass Incarceration Matters:
    Rethinking Crisis, Decline, and Transformation in Postwar American
    History." *Journal of American History* 97, no. 3 (December 2010):
    703–34.

Tumulty, Karen. "Opinion: Where the Hunt for Voter Fraud Is Worse
    Than the Crime Itself." *Washington Post*, February 5, 2019. https://
    www.washingtonpost.com/opinions/where-the-hunt-for-voter-fraud
    -is-worse-than-the-crime-itself/2019/02/05/083bda5e-28c0-11e9
    -984d-9b8fba003e81_story.html?utm_term=.cb53ec4bc88f.

Wachtler, Sol, and David Gould. "Opinion: Fight Voter 'Fraud' Without
    Voter Suppression." *Newsday*, September 16, 2012. https://www
    .newsday.com/opinion/oped/fight-voter-fraud-without-voter
    -suppression-sol-wachtler-and-david-gould-1.4003085.

Permission Credits